Hand Papermaking Traditions of Việt Nam

CONTRIBUTIONS
IN ETHNOBIOLOGY

CONTRIBUTIONS IN ETHNOBIOLOGY

Cynthia Fowler and Steve Wolverton, Series Editors
Cheryl Takahashi, Managing Editor

Contributions in Ethnobiology is a peer-reviewed monograph series presenting original book-length data-rich, state-of-the-art research in ethnobiology. It is the only monograph series devoted expressly to representing the breadth of ethnobiological topics.

Explorations in Ethnobiology: The Legacy of Amadeo Rea
Marsha Quinlan and Dana Lepofsky, Editors

Sprouting Valley: Historical Ethnobotany of the Northern Pomo from Potter Valley, California
James R. Welch

Secwepemc People and Plants: Research Papers in Shuswap Ethnobotany
Marianne B. Ignace, Nancy J. Turner, and Sandra L. Peacock, Editors

Small Things Forgotten: Artifacts of Fishing in the Petén Lakes Region, Guatemala
Prudence M. Rice, Don S. Rice, and Timothy W. Pugh

Ainu Ethnobiology
Dai Williams

Sahnish (Arikara) Ethnobotany
Kelly Kindscher, Loren Yellow Bird, Michael Yellow Bird, and Logan Sutton

Ethnozoology of Egede's "Most Dreadful Monster," the Foundational Sea Serpent
Robert L. France

The Aztec Fascination with Birds: Deciphering 16th-Century Sources in Náhuatl
Eugene S. Hunn

Hand Papermaking Traditions of Việt Nam
James Ojascastro, Veronica Y Phạm, Trần Hồng Nhung, and Robbie Hart

Hand Papermaking Traditions of Việt Nam

James Ojascastro, Veronica Y Phạm, Trần Hồng Nhung,
and Robbie Hart

Society of Ethnobiology

2024

Library of Congress Control Number: 2024924060

ISBN 979-8-9884181-1-5 (paperback)
ISBN 979-8-9884181-2-2 (PDF)

Society of Ethnobiology
Boston University Archaeology Room 345,
675 Commonwealth Ave., Boston, MA 02215

Cover: Nông Thị Đao, a Nùng An papermaker, makes a sheet of dướng (*Broussonetia papyrifera*) paper in Rìa Trên Village, Cao Bằng Province, Việt Nam. Photo by Lê Bích.

Table of Contents

Table of Contents v

List of Figures ix

Acknowledgments xi

1. Background 1

2. Dó (*Rhamnoneuron balansae*) 13
   2.1. Introduction 13
   2.2 Fiber Harvesting 15
   2.3 Papermaking 17
      2.3.1 Fiber Processing 17
      2.3.2 Formation Aid 19
      2.3.3 Papermaking Tools 21
      2.3.4 Sheet Formation 21
      2.3.5 Drying 23
      2.3.6 Recycled Paper 24
   2.4 Toolmakers for Dó Papermaking 24
      2.4.1 Khung Seo Construction 24
      2.4.2 Liễm Seo Construction 25
   2.5 Uses 28
      2.5.1 Painting and Printing 28
      2.5.2 Worship 31
      2.5.3 Royal Edicts 34
      2.5.4 Gilding 36
      2.5.5 Origami 36
   2.6 Current Status 37

3. Dướng (*Broussonetia papyrifera*) 39
   3.1 Introduction 39
      3.1.1 Mường 41
      3.1.2 Nùng 42
   3.2 Fiber Harvesting 42
      3.2.1 Mường Fiber Harvesting 42
      3.2.2 Nùng Fiber Harvesting 43

3.3 Mường Papermaking 44

    3.3.1 Fiber Processing 44

    3.3.2 Formation Aid 45

    3.3.3 Sheet Formation and Drying 45

3.4 Nùng Papermaking 45

    3.4.1 Fiber Processing 45

    3.4.2 Formation Aid 47

    3.4.3 Sheet Formation and Drying 47

3.5 Uses 48

    3.5.1 Writing 49

    3.5.2 Burning 49

    3.5.3 Packaging 49

    3.5.4 Coloring 49

3.6 Current Status 50

4. Dó liệt (*Wikstroemia indica*) 51

4.1 Introduction 51

4.2 Fiber Harvesting 53

4.3 Papermaking 53

    4.3.1 Fiber Processing 53

    4.3.2 Formation Aid 53

    4.3.3 Sheet Formation and Drying 53

4.4 Uses 54

4.5 Current Status 55

5. Haupau (*Linostoma persimile*) 57

5.1 Introduction 57

5.2 Fiber Harvesting 58

5.3 Papermaking 59

    5.3.1 Fiber Processing 59

    5.3.2 Formation Aid 59

    5.3.3 Sheet Formation and Drying 60

5.4 Uses 60

    5.4.1 Burning 60

    5.4.2 Writing 61

5.5 Current Status 61

6. Dó trầm (*Aquilaria crassna*) 63

7. Conservation 67

   7.1 Reinforcing Extant Connections 69

   7.2 Restoring Extinct Connections. 72

   7.3 Creating New Connections. 75

      7.3.1 Origami 75

      7.3.2 Trúc Chỉ and Trucchigraphy 78

   7.4 Botanical Vouchering. 81

8. Conclusion 83

References Cited. 85

Appendix A. 93

Appendix B.. 95

Author Biographies 97

Glossary 99

List of Figures

Figure 1. Geographic occurrences of paper plants, bark harvesting, historic papermaking, and current papermaking in Việt Nam. 5

Figure 2. Phloem fibers used for hand papermaking traditions in Việt Nam. 6

Figure 3. Seven bark-based handmade papers representing five species from Việt Nam. . . . 7

Figure 4. Process of making dó paper 14

Figure 5. Materials for and construction of khung seo 25

Figure 6. Materials for and construction of liểm seo 26

Figure 7. Printing on dó paper 29

Figure 8. Dao Tiển paintings, depicting legendary emperors. 31

Figure 9. Dao Tiển rituals using dó paper 32

Figure 10. Contemporary votive paper, made by machine from wood pulp, printed, and assembled into three-dimensional shapes. 33

Figure 11. Examples of historical and contemporary sắc phong paper. 35

Figure 12. Mường process of making dưởng paper 40

Figure 13. Nùng process of making dưởng paper. 46

Figure 14. Process of making dó liệt paper 52

Figure 15. Process of making haupau paper 58

Figure 16. Harvesting methods of dó trầm (*Aquilaria crassna*) 65

Figure 17. Economy of artisanal papermaking and papercrafts in Việt Nam. 68

Figure 18. Novel plants to consider for bark-based hand papermaking in Việt Nam today. 74

Figure 19. Contemporary artworks using Vietnamese handmade papers 76

Figure 20. Contemporary Trúc Chỉ artworks and processes. 79

Acknowledgments

We extend our deepest gratitude to the many papermakers, bark harvesters, paper artists, and reviewers who have shared with us their wisdom, time, tea, and rượu in support of this work. Many thanks to our dear friends Phan Hải Bằng, Lê Phúc Duy, Dương Văn Quảng, Nguyễn Văn Chúc, Nguyễn Thị Hậu, Nguyễn Văn Hoá, Vương Thị Loan, Nguyễn Ngọc Chiến, Nguyễn Hùng Cường, Nguyễn Anh Nghĩa, Triệu Phúc Thìn, Triệu Văn Thanh, Aimee Lee, and Tim Barrett for their contributions to Vietnamese paper arts and for their continued guidance. Cảm ơn tất cả!

1. Background

Although most paper today is made by machine, some sheets are still made by hand (hereafter "hand papermaking"), following region-specific traditions that may date back centuries. The first paper was made in China with this process over 2 millennia ago, when artisans utilized well-worn rags of wearable clothing made from textiles and barkcloth to prepare pulps for making flat, felted materials intended for writing—i.e., paper (Barrett, 1983; Hunter, 1978; Li et al., 2015; von Hagen, 1943). These rags were spun and woven from raw hemp (*Cannabis sativa* L.), ramie (*Boehmeria nivea* [L.] Gaudich.), and flax (*Linum usitatissimum* L.) fibers; later, papermakers also began preparing pulps directly from raw, unwoven fibers too. Although initially kept a guarded secret, Chinese-style papermaking was soon brought by trade, warfare, and religion to other cultures across Eurasia, whose artisans then experimented with incorporating indigenous flora into this new technology. This experimentation has yielded a remarkable diversity of plant species used in hand papermaking traditions. However, these tend to share similar characteristics, including having: 1) long, cellulose-rich fibers; 2) abundant populations, either naturally or through cultivation; 3) the capacity for rapid and reliable regeneration or reproduction; and 4) insecticidal sap (Boesi, 2016). Together, these four traits are well-represented in plants used in hand papermaking—even among cultures that developed analogous products independent of Chinese contact, like papyrus in Egypt (Bell, 1985) and amate in Mesoamerica (Peters et al., 1987).

With their proximity to and contact with China, hand papermaking traditions across the Asia-Pacific region show strong similarities in both raw materials used and techniques employed. In contrast to papermaking in West Asia and Europe, which sourced paper fiber from mechanically beaten rags woven from the stem fibers of annual herbs (chiefly flax and hemp), papermakers in the Asia-Pacific region mostly employed manually-beaten inner-bark (phloem) fibers of woody perennials, especially those belonging to the plant families Moraceae and Thymelaeaceae (Barrett, 1983; Hunter, 1978; Trier, 1972). Although papermakers, historians, archivists, and ethnobotanists have clearly described these ethnobiogeographic patterns in China, Japan, Korea, and Nepal, they have thus far not done so for the papermaking traditions across mainland Southeast Asia and Austronesia, where paper plants are often misidentified in historical literature (Hunter, 1947; Rantoandro, 1983) and where papermaking traditions—many of which today are endangered (Lee, 2012) or even extinct (Boonpitaksakul et al., 2019; Hunter, 1936)—are still poorly documented. Such is true for the diverse yet understudied papermaking traditions of Việt Nam.

Northern Việt Nam, due to its deep-seated cultural and geographic ties to China, has papermaking traditions with fundamental similarities to others utilized in East Asia. Vietnamese paper (Vietnamese: *giấy*), like paper in China, has also traditionally been produced from the hand-beaten inner bark fibers of moraceous or thymelaeaceous trees, shrubs, or lianas. But the Vietnamese, who were also unwilling subjects of Chinese hegemony and who fought fiercely to maintain their cultural identity despite centuries of political domination by China, manifested this tenacity by co-opting Chinese papermaking techniques (in the first or second century AD), tailoring these methods to their local flora, and, over time, transforming them into traditions unique to Việt Nam (Drège, 1998; Laroque, 2020; Peachey, 1995). Việt Nam was one of the first places to know papermaking, before Nepal (12th century AD; Jnawali, 2019; Trier, 1972), Persia (751 AD; Helman-Ważny, 2014), Tibet (648 AD; Huett, 2020), and Japan (610 AD; Barrett, 1983). This places Vietnamese papermaking contemporary with Korea (108 BC–313 AD; Lee, 2012), and after only China (before 105 BC; Hunter, 1978; Lee, 2012; Tsien, 2004) and Mexico, whose tradition of making amate, a paper analog, dates to at least 74 AD (Benz et al., 2006).

Despite its long history, Vietnamese hand papermaking remains one of the most poorly researched traditions, and the extant literature collectively suffers from three deficiencies: comprehensiveness, botanical accuracy, and graphic documentation. In contrast, recent, detailed, and authoritative monographs and handbooks are available for other papermaking traditions, including general global overviews (Hubbe & Bowden, 2009; Hunter, 1978) and region-specific tomes, including Korea (Lee, 2012), the Himalaya (Arcá, 2010; Imaeda, 1989; Jeanrenaud, 1984; Trier, 1972), Japan (Barrett, 1983), the Tibetan plateau (Helman-Ważny, 2016), Mexico (Peters et al., 1987; von Hagen, 1943), and Europe (Barrett, 2019). No such comprehensive regional reference exists for papermaking in Việt Nam.

Academic and government records available on Vietnamese papermaking traditions document exclusively the industries nearest to Hà Nội, which sourced fiber from a single species (*dó; Rhamnoneuron balansae*). As a result, these records ignore a diversity of other species that are (or have been) used in different regions across northern Việt Nam. The authors of these academic and government records include French officials (Claverie, 1903) and exploring American papermakers during the colonial era (i.e., before 1954; Hunter, 1947), and, more recently, French social scientists (Fanchette, 2016; Fanchette & Stedman, 2009), French paper conservators (Laroque, 2020), and new generations of traveling American papermakers (Koretsky, 2003). Their work is rarely published in the native languages of Việt Nam, which limits local access. To date, few academic publications on Vietnamese hand papermaking have been written by Vietnamese authors, and the contemporary documentation is by journalists in online periodicals printed in Vietnamese using the modern Latin script (Vietnamese: *chữ Quốc ngữ*). This is supplemented by historical documents written in Chinese (Vietnamese: *chữ Hán*) or Vietnamese with Chinese characters (Vietnamese: *chữ Nôm*), which are difficult for most in Việt Nam to access. While valuable, these Vietnamese articles and documents lack essential papermaking and botanical terminology, and consequently neither provide detailed, accurate names of plants, tools, and techniques, nor are they able to compare, contrast, and contextualize Vietnamese papermaking within the broader history and biogeography of East Asian hand papermaking traditions.

In addition, we note that almost no information is available on Vietnamese papermaking between 1954 and 1986, when much of the Indochinese Peninsula was at war. However, despite the absence of over 3 decades of scholarship, it is clear that this period of rapid and drastic change has resulted in the near extinction of Vietnamese hand papermaking traditions.

As a result, the need for a comprehensive synthesis of Vietnamese hand papermaking traditions is urgent, and we provide this monograph—with coauthors including a Vietnamese paper entrepreneur (T.H.N.) and a Vietnamese-American papermaker (V.Y.P.)—as a necessary first step of exploration and documentation, working towards a goal of long-term conservation and restoration of hand papermaking traditions across northern Việt Nam.

A second deficiency we address is the lack of botanical detail and clarity in extant records of Vietnamese papermaking. In many regions, papermaking monographs with adequate botanical detail already exist—written either by ethnobotanists (McClure, 1986; Peters et al., 1987) or by scholars with demonstrable expertise in botany and botanical nomenclature (Barrett, 1983; Helman-Ważny, 2016; Lee, 2012; Trier, 1972). However, no reliable ethnobotanical analog for Vietnamese papermaking has been published, which we attribute to three factors. First, many botanists do not focus on ethnobotany: for example, there is a flora available for Việt Nam, published by a Vietnamese botanist in French, but it is outdated, combined with plant entries for Laos and Cambodia, and contains almost no ethnobotanical information, much less any details on Vietnamese papermaking specifically (Phạm et al., 1992). Second, common names for plants in Vietnamese often reflect usage, so it is not surprising that different species used in Vietnamese papermaking have the same or similar common names. This is especially problematic in the Vietnamese popular media (e.g., Phạm, 2020), where most papermaking plants and their fibers are still called "*dó*" even though this name may be applied to several distinct species. This ambiguity also extends to the plant-based mucilages (Vietnamese: *mò*) used for dispersing fibers on papermaking moulds during sheet formation, the botanical identities of which have been a source of speculation (Laroque, 2020) and only recently determined (Trịnh Bon, personal communication, April 28, 2022). And third, both linguistic and botanical expertise may be deficient: many French records from the colonial era provide common names in Vietnamese for plants allegedly used in Indochinese papermaking, but these reports have neither the botanical nor the linguistic rigor to even connect the reported common names to distinct plant species (Crevost, 1909; Crevost & Lémarié, 1920; Laroque, 2020). In this monograph, we work to overcome these botanical and nomenclatural deficiencies by clarifying and emphasizing regional differences in the species used for both fiber and mucilage, identifying them by both local common names and the scientific names, and explaining in detail where these plants are obtained, how they are processed, and how they are used.

As a final deficiency, we note a lack of quality pictorial and videographic media in the available literature concerning Vietnamese hand papermaking traditions, which exacerbates the confusion, ambiguity, and lack of detail in correctly identifying and documenting the plants, tools, techniques, and locations involved. For example, American papermaker Dard Hunter published photos of his sojourn in Tonkin in what became the first monograph of papermaking in Indochina (Hunter, 1947). However, the quality of these photos does not convey the material and methodological details that set Vietnamese papermaking apart from other East Asian papermaking traditions. Further, Hunter's profession as a foreign papermaker necessarily affected his research focus: while he discusses at length the tools and techniques (often identified using names in English rather than Vietnamese) used by papermakers in villages near Hà Nội, he incorrectly assumes that the tree they used (dó, *Rhamnoneuron balansae*) for papermaking was the same as the shrub (**lokta**, *Daphne bholua*) used to make paper in Nepal—because he never traveled to the areas in Việt Nam where the bark was harvested (Hunter, 1947). Unfortunately, these biases and misidentifications have been parroted in more contemporary publications and media documentation, which similarly lack the supporting pictures and videos of the relevant plants, bark harvesting methods, and paper usage to demonstrate what plants are used (and how they are processed) to make paper (Koretsky, 2003; Prendergast, 2002). And even outside of artisanal papermaking settings, this kind of repeated citation without scrutiny remains a chronic problem in validating anecdotes of plant use in historical ethnobotany (León & Ojascastro, 2024; Łuczaj, 2010). To help clarify this geographic bias and botanical confusion, we provide: 1) detailed pictures to document the diverse plants, tools, and processes used to make paper in Việt Nam; 2) links to online videos to show how Vietnamese artisans transform different plants into paper, woodblocks, and mucilage; and 3) a map (Figure 1) and location descriptions in-text to spatially illustrate where bark harvesting and papermaking are and were practiced across northern Việt Nam. For in-text location descriptions, we use present-day administrative subdivisions used by the Vietnamese government, where Việt Nam is subdivided into provinces (Vietnamese: *tỉnh*), provinces into urban cities (**thành phố**) and rural districts (**huyện**), cities and districts into communes (**xã**), and communes into villages (**xóm** or **bản**); these are also presented, alongside latitude and longitude coordinates, in table format as Appendix A. All figures presented in this monograph are by the first author unless otherwise indicated.

Given these limitations and knowledge gaps, our objectives in publishing this monograph are to provide a literature review and synthesis of previously published articles on Vietnamese papermaking traditions and to supplement—through five detailed and complementary vignettes—current ethnobotanical knowledge concerning the plants, people, and techniques involved in Vietnamese paper arts. These supplements primarily draw from detailed notes,

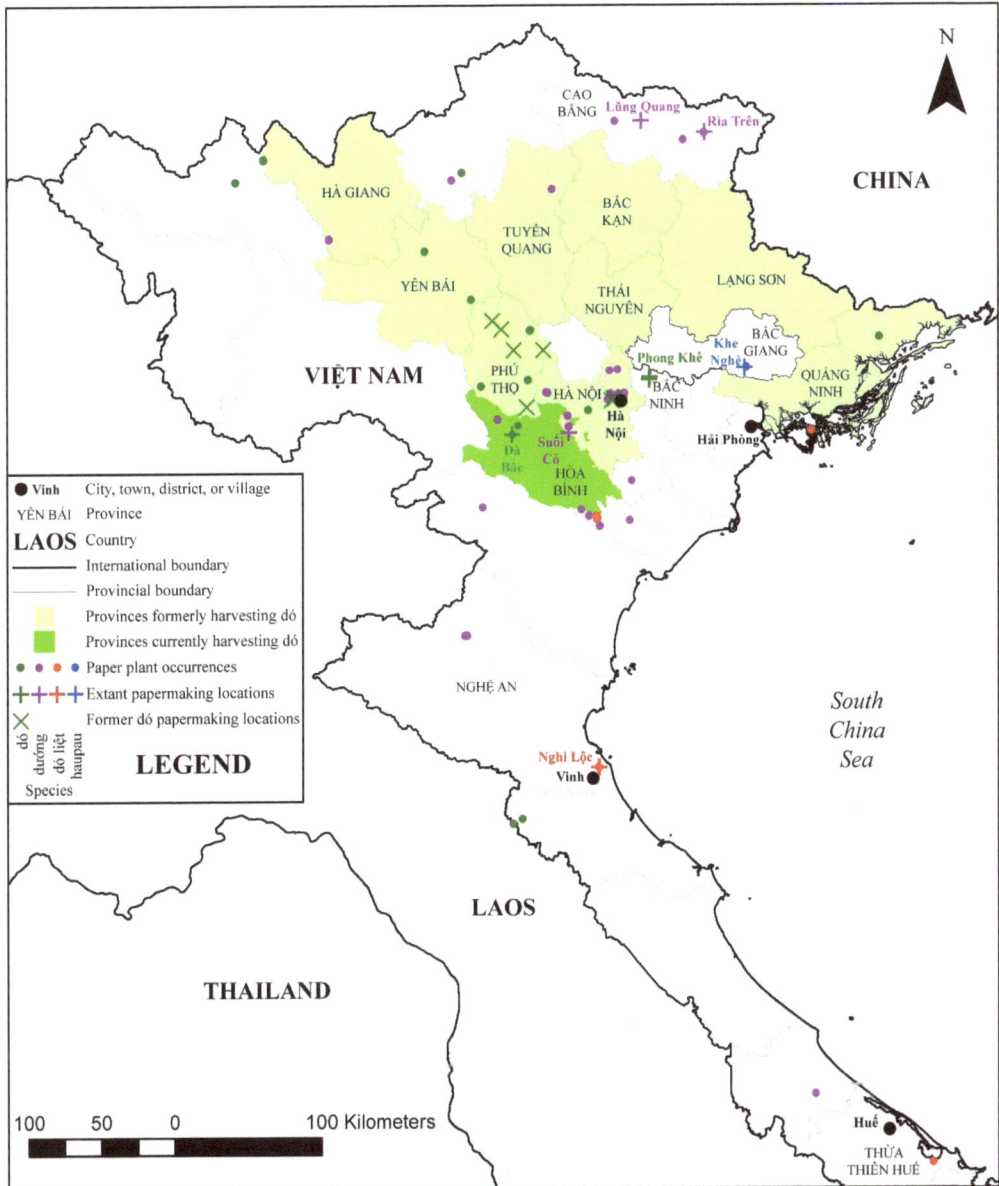

Figure 1. Geographic occurrences of paper plants (•), bark harvesting (shaded provinces), historic paper-making (×), and current papermaking (+) in Việt Nam. Colors correspond to species: green (dó, *Rhamnoneuron balansae*), purple (dướng, *Broussonetia papyrifera*), red (dó liệt, *Wikstroemia indica*), and blue (haupau, *Linostoma persimile*).

pictures, and recordings of semi-structured interviews with bark harvesters, papermakers, and paper artists conducted by the first three authors since January 2019.

Through these interviews, we determined that the inner bark (phloem) of at least four species is still processed into paper in Việt Nam today (Figure 2): **dó** (*Rhamnoneuron balansae* [Maury] Gilg), **dướng** (*Broussonetia papyrifera* [L.] L'Hér. ex Vent.), **dó liệt** (*Wikstroemia*

Figure 2. Phloem (inner bark) fibers used for hand papermaking traditions in Việt Nam. Top to bottom: dó (*Rhamnoneuron balansae*); dưởng (*Broussonetia papyrifera*); dó trầm (*Aquilaria crassna*); haupau (*Linostoma persimile*); and dó liệt (*Wikstroemia indica*).

indica [L.] C.A.Mey.), and **haupau** (*Linostoma persimile* Craib). Of these, only the first two species are still cultivated to a significant degree, with the rest either harvested wild or cultivated only intermittently at present. Our description of the fourth species we cover in this monograph, haupau, represents the first documentation (to our knowledge) of this species as a papermaking plant. A fifth species, ***dó trầm*** (*Aquilaria crassna* Pierre ex Lecomte), has historically been a minor raw material in hand papermaking across tropical Asia (including northern Việt Nam), but its extreme rarity has often precluded its use; we mention this fiber briefly towards the end of this monograph.

By harvesting, cooking, beating, and sheet-forming these bark fibers in different ways, a remarkable diversity of papers can be produced (Figure 3). The profiles in this monograph inevitably fall short of the true diversity of papermaking traditions in Việt Nam: there are

Figure 3. Seven bark-based handmade papers representing five species from Việt Nam. Top left: dó (thin). Top right: dó (thick). Middle left: Nùng dướng. Center: Mường dướng. Middle right: dó liệt. Bottom left: haupau. Bottom right: dó trầm.

likely many more papermaking traditions still practiced across southeastern Asia that remain undocumented by outsiders. Three in particular that deserve more attention are the bamboo papermaking traditions of the Red Dao (Phạm, 2023) and Hmong (Nguyễn, 2023) people, which we felt was beyond our scope as bamboo fibers differ from the bark fibers that form the papers and paper traditions studied here (Ilvessalo-Pfäffli, 1995); and the papermaking tradition of the Raglai people in southern Việt Nam, which ceased practice 50 years ago (Gru Hajan, 2019). With handmade papers (Vietnamese: *giấy thủ công*) now nearly totally displaced by machine-made paper, continued ethnographic study of hand papermaking traditions is an essential first step towards maintaining diverse production of handmade sheets.

In addition to describing the different species whose fibers are used for Vietnamese handmade paper (using both common names in Vietnamese and the Linnaean binomials), we also characterize Vietnamese fiber harvesting practices, the papermaking techniques used, and any associated paper arts traditions, with emphasis on the historically, culturally, and economically dominant paper plant species—dó. At the end of each vignette, we report on the rapid and precipitous decline in the practice of papermaking as a tradition, and at the end of the monograph, we conclude with an urgent call to action to ensure that these ancient and gravely threatened ethnobotanical traditions can continue to be practiced in Việt Nam for future generations.

A note on word choice, style, and usage in this monograph. Within each vignette, the reader will find considerable amounts of specialized terminology, including plant common names, scientific names, and words describing papermaking tools and techniques. We want this publication to be as useful and accessible as possible to the greatest number of people, including botanists, anthropologists, papermakers, paper scholars, paper conservators, government officials, plant conservationists—really anyone interested in this subject matter—so for ease of navigation and comprehension, we have included a glossary at the end to define and clarify the terminology used here. In identifying plants, we refer to them chiefly using the common name in Vietnamese unless indicated otherwise, with italicized scientific names and author abbreviation in parentheses, for example: *thị* (*Diospyros decandra* Lour.). In addition, for plant entries in the glossary, we provide the botanical author abbreviation after the scientific name, followed by a semicolon and the botanical family, for example: *Diospyros decandra* Lour.; Ebenaceae. We also use non-English common names for tools and techniques; these will be referenced in-text without using bold italics except for their first use, where we indicate in parentheses the language of origin, followed by the term in bold italics; for example, when we introduce the term for the Vietnamese screen used in papermaking in-text: (Vietnamese: *liềm seo*). Also, when we refer to the country, we use the requisite accents as following the orthography of the national language (i.e., "Việt Nam") but, when we use the country as a demonym or refer to its national language, we write it following English orthography as "Vietnamese."

Vietnamese naming conventions for people can be complex and confusing to nonnative speakers. One convention is that the family name is written first, followed by one to three (usually two) given names. But unlike most Western cultures, where people are addressed by an honorific and their surname, Vietnamese people are addressed by an honorific and their preferred given name (e.g., the first author would address Nguyễn Văn Thái as "bác Thái", which loosely translates in English to "Mr. Thái"). Aside from better praxis in following Vietnamese custom, electing to refer to key informants we interviewed as "Mr. Nguyễn" would be clumsy and challenging—some 40% of Vietnamese have the surname "Nguyễn" and the reader would get lost trying to determine whether we are referring to Nguyễn Văn Thái, Nguyễn Công Hoàng, or Nguyễn Hùng Cường! Consequently, we elected to refer to people in-text with Vietnamese names with the English honorific equivalent (e.g., Mr., Mrs., Ms., Mx., Dr.), followed by their given name.

Finally, to ensure that this publication concerning Vietnamese people, culture, and traditions is available as a reference for the benefit of people in Việt Nam, we have planned and are currently working on a forthcoming translation into Vietnamese. Regardless of the language in which you find yourself reading this monograph, we hope you find your journey traversing this paper trail as rewarding as we did.

J.O., V.Y.P., T.H.N., and R.H., May 2023

Việt Nam's Paper Plants

2. Dó

Rhamnoneuron balansae (Maury) Gilg
Family Thymelaeaceae

2.1. Introduction

Dó is a shrub or small tree (up to 4 m tall) indigenous to hilly subtropical rainforests of southeastern China, northern Việt Nam, and northeastern Laos. Initially misidentified by French colonial administrators (Crevost, 1907, 1909; Laroque, 2020) as the Himalayan native species *Daphne cannabina* Wall. (now *Daphne bholua* Buch.-Ham. ex D.Don; Prendergast, 2002) or *Daphne involucrata* Wall. (now *Eriosolena involucrata* (Wall.) Tiegh.; Hunter, 1947), dó was later confirmed to be neither of these species and instead placed in its own monospecific genus, *Rhamnoneuron* Gilg (Claverie, 1904; Leandri, 1949). Its leaves are entire, ovate to lanceolate, entire-margined, adaxially glabrous and abaxially sparsely pubescent, often with red petioles and arranged alternately in two ranks along the stem. Perfect, apetalous 4-merous flowers, each bearing a white tubular calyx composed of fused sepals, are borne in terminal, axillary panicles in January (Figure 4a); following pollination, the calyces persist to maturation, enveloping fusiform drupes (Wang et al., 2007).

The dó tree is the chief species used in Vietnamese papermaking, prized because it yields strong, soft paper (Nguyễn, 2002). Although infrequently encountered in the wild today, it is amenable to cultivation for regular harvesting for papermaking. Grown extensively across the foothills of northern Việt Nam during the colonial era expressly for papermaking (Leandri, 1949), its use and cultivation have declined precipitously since, and dó is only known to be cultivated today in the hilly subtropical rainforests of Đà Bắc District, in Hòa Bình Province, and possibly also Chiềng Yên District, in Sơn La Province (Trịnh Bon, personal communication, June 8, 2021). As our field research did not take us to Chiềng Yên, we only report here on dó cultivation and harvest for Đà Bắc District.

Figure 4. Process of making dó paper. a) Flowers of *Rhamnoneuron balansae,* January 2019, Đà Bắc, Hòa Bình, Việt Nam. b) Harvesting history of a *Rhamnoneuron balansae* individual: right, trunk at appropriate harvest size; center, dried xylem decorticated the previous year; left, stump resulting from harvest of both bark and wood. c) Harvesting technique practiced in Đà Bắc, where an incision is made low on the trunk and the bark is carefully peeled from proximal to distal ends. d) Dried and baled dó bark, ready for shipment to papermakers in Bắc Ninh. e) Dó bark rehydrating in a barrel in Bắc Ninh. f) Artisan using a knife to separate the outer and inner layers of dó bark. g) Mixing machine used to homogenize dó fiber slurry after manual beating. h) Artisan making wood shavings of the mò tree, which are then soaked in water to make formation aid. i) Assembly of liềm seo held between top and bottom pieces of khung seo. These are available in four sizes: small (30 cm × 40 cm), medium (40 cm × 60 cm), large (50 cm × 70 cm), and oversize (80 cm × 100 cm). j) Papermaker Nguyễn Thị Độ using a khung seo and liềm seo in dó sheet formation. k) After the post is squeezed free of excess water, sheets are pasted in layers to a porous wall using a dilute tapioca solution. l) Pine-needle brush (chổi lá thông) used for pasting damp dó sheets on the wall. m) Floor fans are used to facilitate drying of dó paper indoors. n) Once dry, the paper stacks are scraped off the walls and peeled apart, layer by layer, to yield finished sheets of dó paper.

2.2 Fiber Harvesting

Dó fiber harvesting used to be practiced by many different ethnic groups in northern Việt Nam, including (but not limited to) the Mường and Kinh (Lê Hồng Kỳ, personal communication, January 2019). A century ago, dó harvesters in Lào Cai, Phú Thọ, Yên Bái, Quảng Ninh, Hòa Bình, Bắc Kạn, and Thái Nguyễn provinces planted and cultivated dó trees on small plantations, each 12–24 ha in size. Though small, these plantations were numerous, covering as much as 750 ha per district (Claverie, 1903). Dó trees grown on such plantations were coppiced at the end of monsoon season (late summer–early fall) and their branches shipped by porter or cart to papermakers in Phú Thọ and Hà Nội (Fanchette & Stedman, 2009). However, with the discontinuation of papermaking in Hà Nội proper by the late 20th century, dó harvesting in the area is now nearly totally extinct (Fanchette & Stedman, 2009). As late as 2009, villages in Lào Cai and Yên Bái provinces were reported to still harvest dó bark for export to papermakers, but whether they still do so is unknown (Fanchette & Stedman 2009). As of 2019, we were able to document only three villages, in Đà Bắc District of Hòa Binh Province, that still harvest dó trees for paper: Bai, Mó Nẻ, and Sưng. They are populated by members of the Dao Tiền people, themselves a branch of the Dao (sometimes spelled Yao) people, one of the 54 ethnic groups recognized by the Vietnamese government.

As observed by the first author in 2019, cultivation of dó in Đà Bắc has not changed very much since the colonial era (Claverie, 1903). One difference, however, is in the propagation method: during French rule, propagation was typically done from seed; these were collected in February and March from ripe, dry, persistent fruits, and were then sown or scattered immediately, as the seeds are recalcitrant (Claverie, 1903). In contrast, the bark harvesters in Đà Bắc today wait for fruits to fall and seeds to germinate of their own accord, transplanting seedlings once they reach a certain size (Triệu Phúc Thìn, personal communication, January 5, 2019). Dó may be grown under a wide variety of conditions, including in backyards, under a forest canopy, on slopes, along roadsides, and among other crops. During the colonial era, young dó seedlings and saplings were shaded from heat and direct sunlight by growing them under woven palm-frond screens or under canopies of mangosteen (*Garcinia* L.), lacquer trees (*Toxicodendron vernicifluum* [Stokes] F.A.Barkley), or various palm trees (Claverie, 1903). In Đà Bắc today, dó is most frequently cultivated instead in fields of *sắn* (cassava, *Manihot esculenta* Crantz; James Ojascastro, personal communication, January 5, 2019) or under *bồ đề* (*Styrax tonkinensis* [Pierre] Craib ex Hartwich) canopies (Nguyễn, 2002). Once it has germinated, dó needs on average 6 to 7 years of growth before it achieves a harvestable size—less (as soon as 3 years) if it is grown in monoculture under open sun, and more (up to 11 years) if it is grown under a closed canopy. According to colonial-era records of dó cultivation, following their first year of growth, dó seedlings were thinned and replanted to a density of about one individual per square meter (Claverie, 1903). Although dó sowing and thinning has nearly completely died out with the widespread disappearance of dó papermaking and bark harvesting, bark harvesters in Đà Bắc have recently revived active dó planting and cultivation to ensure long-term, sustainable regeneration following decades of minimal or nonexistent silviculture (James Ojascastro, personal communication, January 5, 2019).

As the dó trees grow, bark harvesters, both then and now, maximize yield by pruning young branches to encourage the growth of a single, large, straight stem, and both harvesting frequency and intensity have remained about the same since at least the French colonial era. At time of harvest, a tree may be pruned of 5 to 20 branches, each 1–2.5 cm in diameter, for a yield of about 340 g of fresh (130 g dry) bark per tree. Dó trees take at least 3 years to regenerate biomass before they can be harvested again (Claverie, 1903). The highest quality fiber is obtained at the second harvest, when the tree is at least 6 years old; moreover, fiber quality varies by length, with the lowest-quality fiber obtained nearest the root collar, second-quality fiber from the distal portion of the branch, and highest-quality fiber from the section in between (Laroque, 2020). A typical dó tree grown in full sun for fiber could be harvested four times at 3-year intervals over its lifespan; however, after its fourth harvest (as soon as age 12), a tree can yield only a few weak suckers bearing low-quality fiber and is no longer harvested. If left alone, a dó tree may live to the age of 20 or more (Triệu Phúc Thìn, personal communication, January 5, 2019).

North Vietnamese techniques of fiber harvest vary geographically and strongly parallel the patterns seen across Nepal, a similarly mountainous and culturally diverse region with a strong papermaking tradition. In Nepal, three shrubs related to dó, *Daphne bholua* Buch.-Ham. ex D.Don, *D. papyracea* Wall. ex G.Don, and *Edgeworthia gardneri* Meisn., have been used to make a handmade paper called **lokta** for centuries (Trier, 1972). These shrubs are harvested following one of two methods, which we refer to as "branch harvest" and "bark harvest" (Jeanrenaud, 1984; Trier, 1972). In branch harvest, paper plants are coppiced 15–30 cm above the ground—leaving the rootstock intact—and the branches are taken whole back to the village. The bark is then peeled from the severed branches, cooked in alkali, and beaten for making paper, while the xylem is then dried and stored for later use as firewood. This technique was used in in Lào Cai and Yên Bái provinces a century ago but may no longer be extant (Claverie, 1903; Fanchette & Stedman, 2009).

In bark harvest, paper plants are decorticated in situ without clipping the branches. The bark alone is removed, leaving the dying and drying xylem still attached to the rootstock (Figure 4b, c). During the winter months, the persisting dead, dried wood stems are then harvested to burn for cooking and heating. Unfortunately, at least in Nepal, bark harvest frequently proceeds all the way to ground level, which destroys meristematic tissue in the rootstock that could otherwise yield vigorous coppiced growth, resulting in populations of paper plants that are less likely to regenerate (Ghimire & Nepal, 2007; Jeanrenaud, 1984; Yadhav, 2000). Despite its observed risks to Nepalese paper plant populations, bark harvest is the method currently and exclusively used for obtaining dó fiber in Đà Bắc Province. However, the populations of dó trees in Đà Bắc appear healthy, and interviews with Dao Tiến bark harvesters have demonstrated that, during the harvest season, they take into account other qualities on a tree-by-tree basis for optimizing dó tree regeneration post-harvest; these include (but are not limited to) the height along the trunk at which bark can be peeled away, the diameter of the trunk to be harvested, and the age and health of the tree to which the harvested trunk belongs (Triệu Phúc Thìn, personal communication, January 5, 2019).

In Đà Bắc today, dó harvesting is conducted primarily in the cooler months of November and December, when papermakers tend to stock up raw materials and when the bark harvesters have already completed their rice harvest. Some dó fiber is also harvested in July and August (concurrent with other crops), but the summer dó harvest tends to be small because dó bark does not peel readily when the weather is hot (Trần Hồng Nhung, personal communication, February 5, 2022). This seasonality contrasts with colonial records, which report September and October harvests for Lào Cai and Yên Bái provinces (Fanchette & Stedman, 2009). Although dó is on Việt Nam's Red List of Endangered Species (Nguyễn et al., 2007), and wild trees remain scarce, the contemporary cultivation, management, and harvest of dó for papermaking as done at the community level appears to be ecologically sustainable, with vigorous sowing of seed to replace dead trees (James Ojascastro, personal communication, January 5, 2019). Bark harvest in Đà Bắc also still seems to be economically sustainable—albeit modestly so—with harvesters earning anywhere between $8 to 40 USD daily during the harvesting season (Ojascastro, 2023).

After harvest, stripped dó bark must be dried before shipment; this can take anywhere between 2 days and a week, depending on whether it is sunny or raining (Figure 4d). Fresh bark strips are mostly water: 10 kg of fresh bark yield 3 kg of dried bark. Once dried, bark strips are baled into bundles and sold to the few papermakers left in Phong Khê Commune, Bắc Ninh Province (Ojascastro, 2023).

Once a lucrative agribusiness, dó cultivation in northern Việt Nam around 1900 could attain yields as high as 1,140 kg of dried bark per hectare per year (~8,650 harvestable dó trees per hectare per year), and provincial-level bark exports could reach 120 tonnes or more every year (~920,000 dó trees harvested per province per year), with high-quality fiber selling for the 2020 equivalent of $3.45 USD per kilogram (Claverie 1903). Today, Hòa Bình Province harvests little more than 3 tonnes annually, and virtually all of it is sold to the few dó papermakers left in Bắc Ninh Province—at a rate of just 65,000–85,000 Vietnamese đồng (VND), or $2.73–3.57 USD, per kilogram, depending on the season (Ojascastro, 2023).

2.3 Papermaking

2.3.1 Fiber Processing

Historically, dó papermaking occurred seasonally, peaking in early fall when papermakers received their bales of dried bark from dó plantations in Tonkin's highlands. Some mountainous provinces, like Phú Thọ and Hòa Bình, had papermaking industries in the same villages with dó plantations (Claverie, 1903; Triệu Văn Thanh, personal communication, January 5, 2019). Fortunately, a brief but detailed record of papermaking in the highlands is available, through Claverie's 1903 account in Phi Đình Village, Hạ Hòa District, Phú Thọ Province. First, dó bark was soaked for 2 days in water, and then in a lime solution for another 2 days. Thereafter, the lime-impregnated bark was transferred to wooden crosspieces positioned above a cast-iron or copper boiler filled with water; a fire was lit under the boiler, the bark was steamed for a day, and left to cool for another day. On the fifth day, the steamed bark was removed from the boiler setup, washed twice, and beaten with a large mortar-and-pestle. After a third washing, the dó fiber was ready for sheet formation, and proceeded following much the same technique as used today (described in detail below). Unfortunately, the mountain dó papermaking industries in Việt Nam may no longer be extant: although we do not know the fate of the papermaking industries in Phi Đình, we found and interviewed Triệu Văn Thanh, an elderly gentleman in Đà Bắc District, who, in 2019, claimed to be the last living papermaker in Sưng Village; however, he had not made any paper in over 40 years (Triệu Văn Thanh, personal communication, January 5, 2019).

Lowland papermaking industries—specifically those in what is today the sprawling Hà Nội metropolis—thrived as late as the 1970s and 1980s (Peachey, 1995), but ultimately suffered a similar fate as the highland papermaking industries (Trần, 2022). The best-documented example is Yên Thái Village (now part of Tây Hồ District in Hà Nội), famous for making high-quality dó papers since at least the 13th century AD (Peachey, 1995). Artisans here tied dó branches into bundles and immersed them in the Tô Lịch River for 1 to 3 days. Then the bark strips were scraped clean, knots and other defects were pared away, and the strips soaked in limewater for another day. At this point, accounts differ in how Yên Thái fiber processing differs from that of Phi Đình: the limewater-impregnated bark strips were either steamed in earthen ovens for just 8 to 10 hr, or they were cooked in metal double boilers for 3 or 4 days (Claverie, 1903; Fanchette & Stedman, 2009; Hunter, 1947). After steaming or cooking, Yên Thái papermakers used a sharp knife to separate the whitish inner bark from the darker outer bark, with both tissues used to make high-quality and low-quality papers, respectively. The cooked and washed bark was then beaten in large hand- or foot-operated stone mortars before being washed again in bamboo baskets and transferred to a vat for sheet formation (Fanchette & Stedman, 2009; Laroque, 2020).

Although once a thriving craft economy, the handmade paper industries of Yên Thái and its neighbors soon declined to extinction by the 1980s (Trần, 2022). As the Hồng River Valley urbanized in the last decades of the 20th century, Hà Nội absorbed the papermaking craft villages, sterilized them of a centuries-old industry, and transformed them into dense blocks of multi-story concrete apartments, small businesses, boutiques, restaurants, and coffee shops.

The last dó papermaking redoubt in Việt Nam is in Phong Khê Commune of Bắc Ninh Province, where paper has been made by hand since at least 1435 AD (Fanchette & Stedman,

2009). Papermakers here are ethnic Kinh, who are the dominant (85% of the population) ethnic group in Việt Nam. In Phong Khê, just three villages keep this 600-year-old tradition alive: Đào Xá, Châm Khê, and Dương Ổ.

At Dương Ổ—the most renowned of the extant dó papermaking villages—paper is made throughout the year. Bales of dó bark are purchased in bulk during the harvesting season and stored in dry conditions until they can be processed (Figure 4d). As in Yên Thái, the papermaking process in Dương Ổ begins with rehydrating dried dó bark in tubs of water for 3 days (Figure 4e), then subjecting the rehydrated bark strips to a cursory pass of scraping to remove toughened fibers and loose debris (Figure 4f). Here, the Dương Ổ artisans condense some steps, boiling the bark directly in a cauldron of 12% limewater for 2 days until the bark strips are soft enough to be pulled apart with bare hands. After cooking, the bark is rinsed through mesh repeatedly to purge the lime. Then the Dương Ổ papermakers separate the inner and outer bark, but the latter is now usually discarded as its poor quality renders it no longer profitable to process. Bark beating is first done over the course of several days with wooden mallets upon stones or wooden boards (as traditionally done for centuries), and then processed further in a Hollander beater (Trần, 2022) or similar mixing or pulping machine (Figure 4g). The Hollander beater, designed in Holland over 4 centuries ago, consists of a racetrack-shaped basin and a rotor armed with blades along its circumference (Barrett, 2019). Hand-beaten fiber and water are added to the basin, the rotor is turned on, and then the slurry spins around the track and under the spinning rotor, which cuts the fibers to shorter lengths. Once the suspension of fiber pulp (Vietnamese: *lê*) is homogenous, it is picked free of bark flecks and other debris and then dispersed in a large vat of water; this action—adding pulp to a vat and stirring it until uniformly distributed—is called charging.

2.3.2 Formation Aid

Before sheets can be made, a key ingredient must be added to the aqueous fiber suspension: formation aid, a viscous, slippery mucilage that slows drainage of water from a papermaking mould so that the papermaker has enough time to tilt and shake the mould to yield a wet paper sheet of uniform texture and thickness. Formation aid can be made from a variety of materials: in the Western Hemisphere, when employed, it is usually synthetic and made by mixing either polyethylene oxide or polyacrylamide powder in water, while in Eastern traditions, it is usually extracted by soaking parts of plants (e.g., in Japan the pounded root of **tororo-aoi**, *Abelmoschus manihot* [L.] Medik.) in water until it becomes mucilaginous (Barrett, 1983). In the case of dó papermaking, formation aid is derived from the wood of a tree called **mò** (Figure 4h). Papermakers at Dương Ổ today (and in Yên Thái historically) import their mò as short (~1 m long) logs from Tuyên Quang Province, while the Đà Bắc papermakers (when they were still active, i.e., before 1980) harvested their mò trees locally from the surrounding forest.

The exact species identity of mò has long been enigmatic. Most frequently, mò was reported as a woody shrub in the genus *Clerodendrum* L., usually *C. trichotomum* Thunb. (Fanchette, 2016; Laroque, 2020), which belongs to the Lamiaceae (mint) family. Alternatively, it was identified as a tree in the genus *Litsea* Lam. (Crevost & Lémarié, 1920; Huard & Durand, 1954; Laroque, 2020; Peachey, 1995), a member of the Lauraceae (laurel) family. To clarify this uncertainty, we solicited assistance from Vietnamese wood expert Trịnh Bon. Mr. Bon examined samples of fresh wood currently used to make formation aid for dó papermaking, and he determined the following: the wood used in Bắc Ninh to make formation aid was *Litsea monopetala* (Roxb.) Pers., while the mucilage used in Đà Bắc came from the wood of *bời lời*, *Litsea glutinosa* (Lour.) C.B.Rob. (Trịnh Bon, personal communication, April 28, 2022). No physical evidence was found pointing to *Clerodendrum* as a current mucilage source. Furthermore, the first author (J.O.) immersed woody *Clerodendrum trichotomum* branches—pruned by Missouri Botanical Garden botanist Andrew Townesmith from an escaped population in Arkansas—in water and failed to obtain any mucilage from any of the stem tissues. Further calling the identification of mò as *Clerodendrum* into question, we have not found other claims of species in Lamiaceae used as formation aids in any other hand papermaking tradition. By comparison, the use of Lauraceae for producing mucilage already has precedent, in both hand papermaking traditions (e.g., in China, where *Machilus thunbergii* Siebold & Zucc. is used as a formation aid for making xuan calligraphy paper; McClure, 1986; Mullock, 1995) and in culinary traditions (e.g., in Louisiana Creole cuisine, where sassafras—as filé powder—is used to thicken stews like gumbo).

To obtain formation aid from the mò tree, papermakers use a spokeshave to first decorticate the mò logs, and then shave the barkless wood into thin strips (Figure 4h). Next, the shavings are soaked in a bucket of water overnight, turning it mucilaginous. The mucilage is then strained through a mesh, such as mosquito netting, to remove the mò wood strips. The strained mucilage is then added to the papermaking vat and whisked with a bamboo rod until the desired consistency is obtained (James Ojascastro, personal communication, January 14, 2019). According to colonial records, about 1 part mò shavings are needed per 30 parts of dó bark, weight for weight (Claverie, 1903).

Koretsky (2003) reported a wetland bush (Vietnamese: *gáo nước*) as a source of formation aid for dó papermaking in Đống Cao Village, Bắc Ninh, about 2 decades ago. Bark from this species was placed in a basket, immersed in a pond for some time, and later retrieved, thus yielding copious amounts of mucilage for papermaking. Since no fresh gáo nước was shown in Koretsky's documentary, we were unable to conclusively identify the plant associated with this Vietnamese vernacular name. One Vietnamese plant called gáo nước is the buttonbush *Cephalanthus tetrandra* (Roxb.) Risdale & Bakh.f. in the Rubiaceae (coffee) family, but neither this nor any of its confamilials are known sources of formation aid in any hand papermaking tradition. Further interviewing and subsequent plant vouchering is therefore needed to correctly identify the mucilage plant used in Đống Cao Village.

2.3.3 Papermaking Tools

Dó papermakers past and present use a papermaking technique (Vietnamese: *seo*; Figure 4i) similar to the methods of sheet formation used primarily in Japan and Korea (Japanese: *nagashizuki*; Korean: *ssangbal tteugi*; Barrett, 1983; Lee, 2012). But before we describe the methodology, we must first introduce the specialized tools used in Eastern papermaking traditions to provide some geographic and cultural context. In Japan, nagashizuki relies on a special kind of mould with two components: a frame (Japanese: *keta*) made from *hinoki* (*Chamaecyparis obtusa* [Siebold & Zucc.] Endl.) wood, and a screen (Japanese: *su*) made from very thin bamboo splints sewn together with horsehair (Hunter, 1978) or silk (Barrett, 1983) which permits drainage of water but not passage of fiber pulp. The keta is fashioned from two frames hinged together like a clamshell; during sheet formation, the two frames hold the su in place and are secured by means of (usually two) latches, forming a single unit (Japanese: *sugeta*).

The Vietnamese keta counterpart (Vietnamese: *khung seo*) is also composed of two frames, but they are usually unhinged and fully separable, such that the bamboo screen (Vietnamese: *liêm seo*) between the two khung seo pieces (Figure 4i) is secured using pressure from the hands. The bottom frame has ribs running parallel to the short dimension to support the liêm seo, structurally analogous to the one-piece and unhinged screen support (Korean: *bal teul*) made from wood of lacebark pine (Korean: *baeksong*; *Pinus bungeana* Zucc. ex Endl.) that is indigenous to Korea for Korean-style sheet formation (Korean: *webal tteugi*). The top piece of the khung seo is a simple wooden U-shape, with the free ends of the "U" fixed in place with a bamboo spacer bar.

In contrast to the different structures of the papermaking frames described above (Japanese keta, Korean bal teul, and Vietnamese khung seo), the corresponding papermaking screens (su, bal, and liêm seo, respectively) are quite similar in structure, all constructed from thin, uniformly sized bamboo splints that are woven together with horsehair, silk, nylon, or monofilament threads and tied along the long edges to narrow pieces of wood or bamboo—called edge sticks—that serve as a handle for the papermaker to hold while couching wet sheets onto a post. Across Japanese, Korean, and Vietnamese screens, the splints themselves are essentially identical in construction (see below), but the edge sticks, however, differ in shape and material: those of the su and bal are flattened and made of either wood (su) or bamboo (bal), while the liêm seo edge stick is round and fashioned from two longitudinally bisected halves of a bamboo rod, which are tied on either side of the knotted end of the screen with cotton thread. Greater detail on the makers and materials responsible for both khung seo and liêm seo construction is provided below, under section 2.4.

2.3.4 Sheet Formation

To form dó sheets, the papermaker grips the two pieces of the khung seo firmly around the liêm seo, and then as a unit, swings them with a scooping motion into a vat filled with water, beaten fibers, and formation aid (Figure 4j). In Yên Thái, the far side of the mould was dipped into the vat first, but today in Dương Ổ the technique more resembles Japanese nagashizuki, with the near side of the mould being immersed (Barrett, 1983; Hunter, 1978). Once the mould is scooped into the vat (Vietnamese: *bể seo*) to fill the surface with fiber and formation aid solution, it is held horizontally just above the vat surface and gently shaken side to side and front to back to even the sheet as the excess water drains through and fiber is accumulated on the surface of the liêm seo. This motion resembles in miniature the side-to-side arcing movements (Korean: *yupmuljil*) in webal tteugi, but contrasts with the vigorous front-to-back sloshing typical of nagashizuki. The papermaker may then briefly "float" the liêm seo—which is still pinned between the two khung seo pieces—on the vat solution surface to further shake and wash any loose fibers into place; this step also may help reduce adhesion between the liêm seo and the wet paper so it can be couched (see below) more easily (Koretsky, 2003).

For very large sheets of dó (1 m across or more), additional support is needed due to the weight and size of the khung seo. Artisans who make big sheets of dó paper, like Nguyễn Chí Cười and Ngô Thị Thanh in Bắc Ninh, have flexible overhead brackets installed above the bể seo, allowing for the suspension and easier manipulation of large and heavy khung seo. A similar method is used for large sugeta in Japan (Barrett 1983; Red Trillium Press, 2009). Based on known introductions of nagashizuki from Japan to Korea (especially during Japanese occupation, 1910–1945; Lee, 2012), it is possible that suspended seo technique could have been introduced recently from Japan.

The steps that follow, between sheet formation and sheet drying, share many similarities with those in Japan and Korea (Barrett, 1983; Lee, 2012). Following the formation of a sheet, the khung seo is moved out of the way, and the liêm seo is deftly lowered, paper side down, onto a moist sheet of fabric, leaving the wet paper sheet in between. The bottom edge of the liêm seo is flicked up and then the entire liêm seo is deftly removed, leaving the wet paper sheet adhered to the fabric. This process of paper deposition, called couching in European papermaking, is repeated, stacking wet sheets of paper directly onto each other until the desired number of paper sheets have been accumulated. In Việt Nam, sheets are couched in the same manner from sheet to sheet; this contrasts with the Korean tradition, in which hanji is couched with the bal rotated 180 degrees each time, to alternate between sheets the slightly uneven distribution of fiber (thicker along the edge near the papermaker, and thinner along the edge opposite the papermaker) caused by the motion of webal tteugi (Lee, 2012). Once the desired number of sheets are formed and couched, the stack, or post, of paper is covered with another damp piece of fabric and placed into a press to expel excess water, as in Japan (Barrett, 1983) and Korea (Lee, 2012). In Japan, Korea, and Việt Nam, pressure can be exerted in different ways: the traditional and more antiquated method is by means of a long lever weighted at the end by stones, while modern techniques make use of either a screw (Hunter, 1947; Koretsky, 2003) or a hydraulic press (Lee, 2012), used to incrementally increase pressure as excess water drains from the post. The time needed for pressing may vary, from 30 min (Koretsky, 2003) to 12 hr (James Ojascastro, personal communication, January 7, 2019).

After pressing, the still-damp sheets can be separated from one another. This is done carefully, starting at one corner and gently peeling each sheet one at a time from the rest of the stack. Once detached, the sheet is flipped over and gently swept with a soft-bristled brush to remove any stray fibers and then transported in stacks to spacious concrete rooms and stairwells for drying.

2.3.5 Drying

In Việt Nam, which receives copious amounts of rain throughout the year, drying paper is challenging. In Yên Thái, sheets were traditionally dried slowly outside (draped individually on bamboo rods and suspended on racks), or quickly indoors (each sheet pasted, using a brush dipped in a runny solution of mò, for a few seconds on an oven-heated, wall-mounted metal plate) (Hunter, 1947; Laroque, 2020); this latter technique is still practiced today in the Himalaya (Fanchette & Stedman, 2009), Japan (Barrett, 1983), China (Mullock, 1995), and Korea (Lee, 2012). But in Việt Nam today, newly formed sheets of dó paper—whether by seo or nagashizuki—are dried using a third technique: papermakers in Phong Khê begin the drying process by pasting short stacks of pressed sheets of dó paper onto porous, unheated concrete walls (Figure 4k) using a triangular brush made from pine needles (Vietnamese: *chổi lá thông*; Figure 4l)—a tool also used for the same purpose in parts of China (Tomasko, 2004). To begin each drying stack, the papermaker first dips the chổi lá thông in a runny tapioca solution (Vietnamese: *nước hồ*)—i.e., sắn (cassava) starch (Vietnamese: *hồ*) dissolved in water—to paste a large, thick scrap sheet of dó on the concrete wall. Then, without using the tapioca solution, the papermaker pastes a wet, pressed sheet of dó onto the scrap sheet. The next pressed sheet of dó is brushed—again without the tapioca solution—onto the first pressed sheet, and this process repeated until the scrap sheet has 40 pressed sheets adhered to it. At this point, the papermaker dips the chổi lá thông into the tapioca solution a second time to paste another large thick scrap piece of dó onto the stack, covering the pressed sheets completely and sealing the stack to the wall. This process is repeated until the entire wall is pasted with short stacks of dó paper; this scales to as many as 6,000 dó sheets per drying room at any given time. Once the room is filled wall-to-wall with damp paper stacks, the papermakers orient oscillating floor fans facing the paper stacks to evaporate moisture away from the paper (Figure 4m). Drying time varies depending on season: paper takes 10 days of fan-drying during the wet summers but dries in half that time during the drier winters. Three-day expedited drying is possible if the Dương Ổ papermakers turn on the air conditioning, but this happens sparingly due to the cost of electricity. Once the paper stacks are completely dry, the scrap cover paper is removed, the sheets are peeled apart again (Figure 4n), and the finished paper is then baled and sold inside Việt Nam or exported abroad—mostly to France.

2.3.6 Recycled Paper

Recycling—also traditionally done by hand—has also played a major role in the paper economy of Việt Nam. This process starts by re-pulping scrap dó paper in water. Unlike papers made directly from dó bark, recycled pulp is formed into sheets with a mould consisting of a stretched porous screen but no deckle (Koretsky, 2003), very similar to the sheet-forming tools used by Nùng papermakers to make dướng paper (see subsequent vignette). The mould is dipped quickly into the vat of recycled fiber and couched onto a post, but with woven cotton rags interleaved between each fresh sheet of recycled paper. The post is then pressed using the same techniques (weighted lever or screw press) as non-recycled handmade paper, albeit with less pressure. After pressing, recycled handmade sheets are peeled apart, draped over bamboo rods, and hung to dry on racks (Koretsky, 2003). Once dry, recycled dó paper—which is considered lower quality—tends to be used for packaging (Vietnamese: **giấy khan**) or in burning rituals (see section "2.5 Uses" below).

2.4 Toolmakers for Dó Papermaking

In this aside, we revisit in greater detail the handmade tools used in dó papermaking, with emphasis on their makers and the raw materials employed.

2.4.1 Khung Seo Construction

Like bespoke paper itself, artisanal papermaking tools around the world are likewise made by hand by a select few craftspeople—and Việt Nam is no exception. For example, the only artisan who still makes khung seo today is a man named Nguyễn Công Hoàng, a carpenter who lives in Châm Khê Village, Phong Khê Commune, Bắc Ninh Province. Although most of his income from the past 40 years has come from making and selling wooden furniture, Mr. Hoàng also has 30 years of experience making khung seo, a skill he perfected learning from his elder brother, who is now retired and no longer makes khung seo. Mr. Hoàng is now the only artisan still making khung seo for dó papermakers, but he says he has some apprentices learning the craft at his workshop that will carry on this tradition after he retires. Building a khung seo requires a minimum of 2 years' experience in carpentry, and mastering khung seo manufacture takes several years more. For an experienced carpenter like Mr. Hoàng, it takes about 1 week to make a single khung seo, which are tailored to the papermaker's desired size (Figure 5a); the largest of these measure 80 cm by 100 cm, and, due to their size, are hinged like a clamshell (Figure 5b; Nguyễn Công Hoàng, personal communication, 2022).

To build khung seo, Mr. Hoàng uses two raw materials: wood from a *Magnolia* Plum. ex L. tree called **dổi** (Figure 5c) for perimeter of both the top (Figure 5d) and bottom (Figure 5e) pieces, and **mai** or **luồng** (*Dendrocalamus* Nees; Figure 5f) bamboo for the wedge-shaped

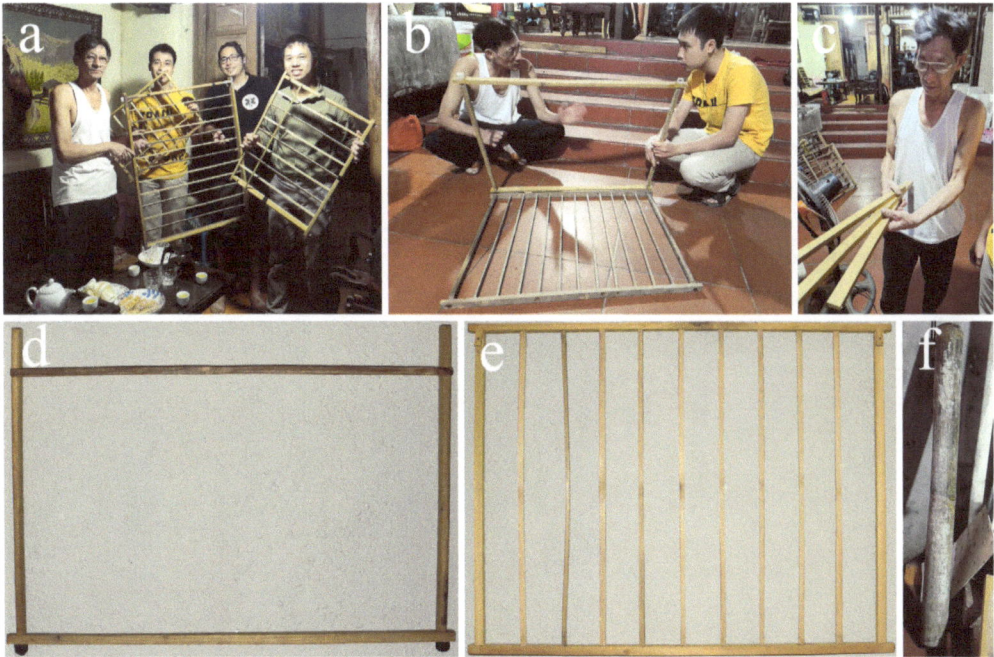

Figure 5. Materials for and construction of khung seo. a) Nguyễn Công Hoàng and visitors showing off small, medium, and large khung seo he made. b) Mr. Hoàng discussing with origami artist Nguyễn Hùng Cường construction of the largest khung seo (foreground), which unites the top and bottom frames with a hinge to form a clamshell structure, akin to the Japanese keta. It measures 80 cm × 100 cm. c) Mr. Hoàng showing pieces of dỗi (*Magnolia* sp.) lumber, which he uses for the outer frames of the khung seo. d) Top piece of khung seo; note the U-shape, with the bamboo spacer bar holding the free ends at a constant width. e) Khung seo, bottom piece, showing nine mai (*Dendrocalamus* sp.) ribs held in place by a frame made of dỗi (*Magnolia* sp.) wood. f) Dried mai (*Dendrocalamus* sp.) bamboo culm used for the parallel ribs spaced in the center of the bottom khung seo frame.

ribs on the interior of the bottom piece that support the liềm seo. He says dỗi is the preferred wood for khung seo because it is extremely warp-resistant, and it can tolerate repeated and extensive immersion in water without losing structural integrity: a khung seo made with dỗi wood can be used to make over half a million sheets of dó paper over a typical 3-year lifespan with constant use. However, this water resistance comes at considerable expense: dỗi wood costs four times as much, volume for volume, as the hinoki wood used for Japanese keta. Since Mr. Hoàng lives in an urbanized area, neither dỗi nor mai grow nearby and he must purchase both from traveling dealers, who have visited less frequently since the COVID-19 pandemic began.

2.4.2 Liềm Seo Construction

As with the case of khung seo, just one man, a former papermaker from Xuân Đỉnh, Từ Liêm District (now part of Hà Nội) named Nguyễn Văn Thái, still makes liềm seo today (Figure 6a).

Figure 6. Materials for and construction of liềm seo. a) Nguyễn Văn Thái (right) explaining liềm seo construction with Mr. Cường, using a completed example (foreground). Chain lines on Mr. Thái's liềm seo measure between 17 and 18 mm apart. b) Fresh tre splints. c) Tre splints after their first immersion in a củ nâu (*Dioscorea cirrhosa*) dyebath. d) Intact củ nâu tubers and corresponding red-brown dyebath filled with water and chopped củ nâu tubers. e) Mr. Thái holding tre splints after full treatment involving smoking and two dyebaths. f) Nylon monofilament fishing line Mr. Thái uses to stitch tre splints together to form liềm seo. g) Dumbbell-shaped weights used to keep the monofilament taut against each splint during liềm seo construction. h) Mr. Thái using a loom to weave the monofilament chain lines around each splint to make a liềm seo.

Since Mr. Hoàng and Mr. Thái make different parts of a tool designed to work together, it is not surprising that they are friends and that they share many similarities—in fact, they consider each other brothers, though they live in different villages and are not related by blood or marriage. Both lost their fathers when they were 15 years old, and their mothers are the same age. Their working relationship is so steadfast that Mr. Thái cannot even remember how long they have been collaborating. What Mr. Thái does remember is his personal connection to liềm seo: mentored by his parents and siblings, Mr. Thái first started making liềm seo at the age of 3; by age 12, he had mastered the craft. Although Xuân Đỉnh and adjacent Xuân La (both now part of Hà Nội) were craft villages famous for centuries up until the mid-1900s for the manufacture of liềm seo, Mr. Thái is the only craftsperson left still practicing this trade today, and though some of his siblings who tutored him are still alive, they are now too old to make liềm seo. In any case, most of Mr. Thái's income comes from elsewhere; most days, he works in electronics, building, repairing, and maintaining appliances and telecommunications equipment. With the Vietnamese economy now more digitized and globalized, Mr. Thái's son trained instead in electrical engineering, and the future of liềm seo manufacture is now uncertain. Fortunately, Mr. Thái reports that he has a few apprentices learning different aspects of liềm seo construction, but that none of them have yet mastered the craft in its totality (Nguyễn Văn Thái, personal communication, November 9, 2022).

The principal raw material for liềm seo are 3- or 4-year-old culms of bamboo (Vietnamese: *tre*) harvested in and imported from Thanh Trì, immediately south of Hà Nội. At time of publication, the authors were unable to see these "tre" bamboos in situ and so they could not provide a species determination; however, given that henon (Japanese: *hachiku*; *Phyllostachys nigra* var. *henonis*; Asao Shimura, personal communication, December 3, 2022) is used for making su in Japan and *wangdae* (*Phyllostachys reticulata* (Rupr.) K.Koch; Aimee Lee, personal communication, December 16, 2022) is used for making bal in Korea, and that there are several species of *Phyllostachys* natively present in Việt Nam (Trần, 2010), we speculate that the "tre" Mr. Thái uses for making liềm seo may also be a species of *Phyllostachys*. Although any part of the tre culm may be used to make liềm seo, tissue on the exterior (Vietnamese: *cật*) is tougher and tighter-grained than tissue on the inside, and so the highest quality liềm seo is made exclusively from the former. Because Mr. Thái, who is meticulous and uncompromising, uses only 100% cật, this means that all currently made liềm seo are of this tissue.

To process cật tissue from tre culms into thin splints, Mr. Thái splits the bamboo into thinner and thinner pieces using a knife. Once the bamboo pieces approach the desired thinness, Mr. Thái feeds them, one by one, through a metal drawplate with a tiny hole in the center, to produce thin, flexible splints of uniform diameter (Figure 6b). However, to maximize the lifespan of the resulting liềm seo, the splints need additional processing to confer water and insect resistance; this is accomplished by first dyeing the splints (Figure 6c) in a bath of chopped *củ nâu* (*Dioscorea cirrhosa* Lour.) tubers (Figure 6d), then smoking them over a fire, and finally dyeing them once more with củ nâu. Once dry, the once-smoked and twice-dyed bamboo splints—now deep red-brown in color (Figure 6e)—are ready to be woven together, which Mr. Thái accomplishes with aid from a special loom. This stitching—which forms the chain lines of the screen—has varied materially over time, from horsehair (Hunter,

1978) to silk thread (Nguyễn Văn Thái, personal communication, November 9, 2022). Then, in 1985, Japanese artisan papermaking entities, seeking cheaper but durable alternatives to domestic su, looked to Việt Nam, and inquired if the liềm seo makers could make bamboo screens for export—but woven with nylon monofilament fishing line (Figure 6f) in place of silk or horsehair. The substitution stuck, and Mr. Thái has made liềm seo with fishing line ever since.

Regardless of whether horsehair, silk thread, or nylon monofilament is used, each chain line in a bamboo screen begins by bisecting a long length of the weaving material, securing the midpoint to the loom, and spooling the ends around small, dumbbell-shaped stone weights (Figure 6g). Splints are then added one by one, and weaving proceeds by the formation of tiny woven chains around each splint as stones are alternated from one side of the loom to the other (Figure 6h). Mr. Thái repeats these steps hundreds (sometimes thousands!) of times until the woven screen achieves the desired width. Once long enough, Mr. Thái knots the ends of the monofilament, hides the working ends between two pieces of a bisected bamboo shoot (i.e., the edge sticks) that comprise the liềm seo handle and ties the handle to the completed liềm seo using cotton thread. Once the edge sticks are secured in place, Mr. Thái neatly trims the fishing line and splints to uniform lengths to round out the final touches.

2.5 Uses

Historically, dó paper played an integral role across many aspects of Vietnamese culture, including for writing, painting, woodblock printing, packaging, ritual burning, and the manufacture of fireworks. However, over the last 4 or 5 decades, political, social, and economic forces have together rapidly pushed Việt Nam's centuries-old papermaking and paper arts traditions to the brink of extinction, strangling some uses and extinguishing others. But as globalization blends new ideas with old traditions, it has inspired young Vietnamese designers to take advantage of dó and other handmade Vietnamese papers as a novel medium for many kinds of contemporary arts from around the world.

2.5.1 Painting and Printing
Perhaps the most famous and uniquely Vietnamese use of dó paper is its role in Đông Hồ paintings (Figure 7a). Named for the village outside of Hà Nội where they have been made since the 11th century, Đông Hồ paintings depict allegorical and auspicious icons of Vietnamese folk tales, such as babies, carp, roosters, and pigs. The paintings are sold or gifted to bestow good luck and prosperity during special occasions, such as weddings and the *Tết* holiday (Vietnamese Lunar New Year).

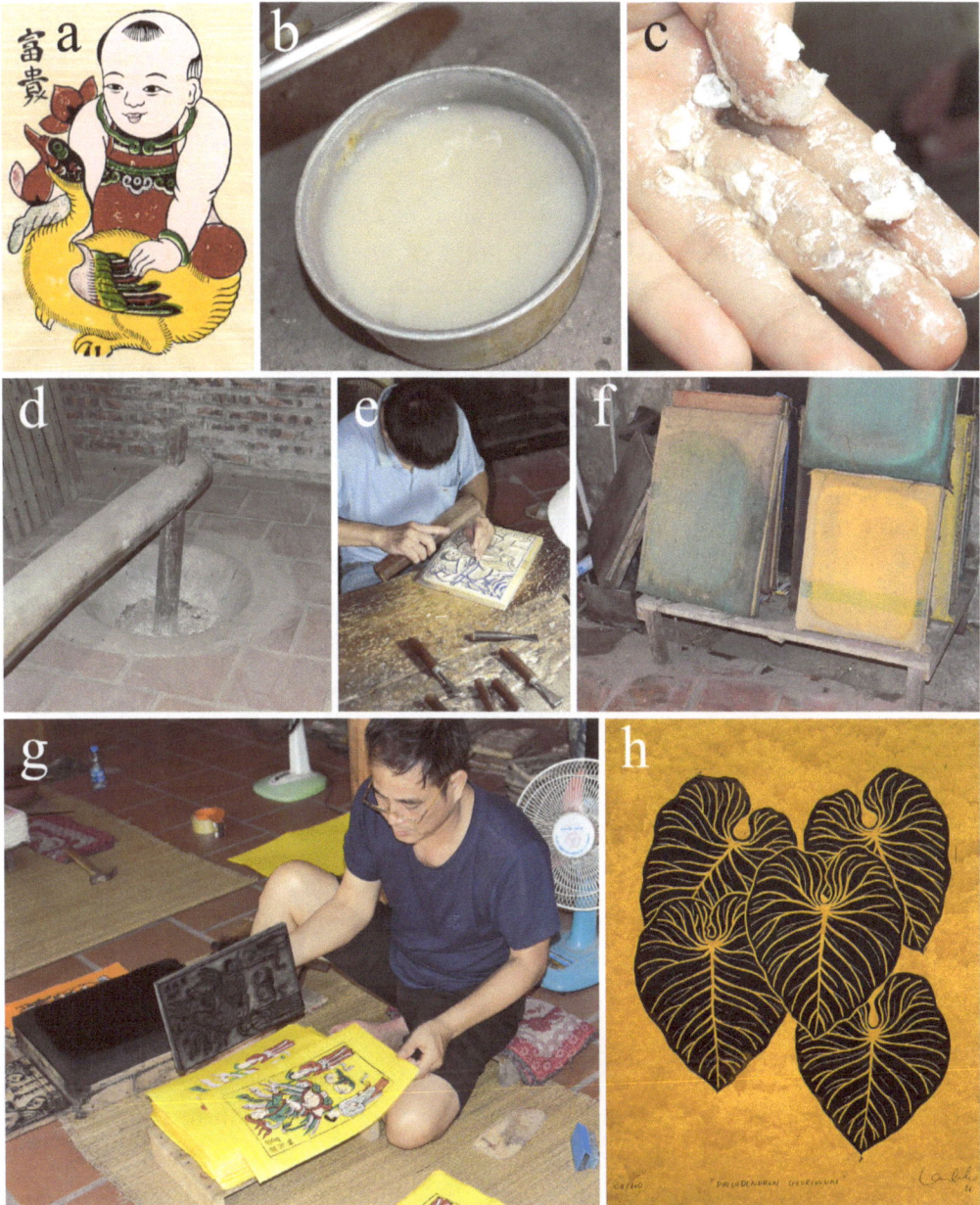

Figure 7. Printing on dó paper. a) Typical Đông Hồ painting. b) Fermenting sticky rice in water. c) Crushed seashells. d) Mortar and pestle for crushing seashells. e) Artisan carving color blocks from thị (*Diospyros decandra*) wood. f) Ink pads made from stretched canvas. g) Artisan printing the black color—made from soot obtained by burning bamboo leaves—onto giấy điệp to complete a Đông Hồ painting. h) "Philodendron gloriosum" by Huỳnh Lân, modern blockprint on sắc phong (royal) dó paper, 2021.

Like with papermaking in Phong Khê, globalization and industrialization transformed the artisanal economy of Đông Hồ Village. Previously, Đông Hồ was composed almost entirely of a cooperative that painted icons by hand. But as the market opened, artisans found it more and more challenging to continue their livelihoods making Đông Hồ paintings, and many left the industry. By 1988, the Đông Hồ painting cooperative ended, leaving only Nguyễn Đăng Chế and his family to keep the tradition alive (Peachey, 1995).

Although they are still called Đông Hồ "paintings," this is now a misnomer: painted icons are too prohibitively expensive to sell today, and the "paintings" currently sold are instead mass-produced as woodcuts from hand-carved blocks. Nevertheless, the process of making Đông Hồ images begins today as it did centuries ago: by whitening dó paper, which is naturally straw-colored. Rather than using bleach, Đông Hồ artisans begin by fermenting sticky rice in water (Figure 7b); the resulting alcoholic slurry prevents organic colorants used for the Đông Hồ paintings from rotting before application. After about 5 days of fermentation, the starchy liquid is mixed in a 70:30 ratio with finely pulverized, decomposed seashells (Figure 7c, d) imported from Hạ Long Bay in Quảng Ninh Province (Peachey, 1995) to yield a milky slurry. The slurry is then brushed with a chổi lá thông onto sheets of dó paper, which turn chalky white upon drying. The treated dó paper, now called painting paper (Vietnamese: **giấy in tranh**) or seashell paper (Vietnamese: **giấy điệp**), is then ready for painting or printing, using vegetable- or mineral-based dyes or pigments mixed in glutinous rice water.

To make Đông Hồ "paintings" today, artisans begin by drawing a multicolored image on paper as it would appear in finished form. The image is then decomposed into monochromatic layers (usually six or fewer) which, when printed in a particular order on the same sheet of paper, reconstitute the initial picture. Each layer is traced onto a wooden (Vietnamese: **gỗ**) slab of **thị** (*Diospyros decandra* Lour.) and then chiseled according to the tracing (Figure 7e). Đông Hồ artisans use only gỗ thị for woodblock printing because it is soft enough to be chiseled with ease but flexible enough to resist splitting for thin, detailed incising. Blocks are colored by pressing them on burlap pads (Figure 7f), which are saturated with the colorant of choice. Once inked, blocks are printed sequentially on a sheet of whitened dó paper, with subsequent colors applied once the paint from the preceding print has dried (Figure 7g). Once all the necessary wooden blocks ("color blocks") are carved for a given image, the Đông Hồ artisans can produce 400 or 500 prints per day (Nguyễn Ngọc Chiến, personal communication, August 17, 2019). Although the village sells prints throughout the year, especially to visiting tourists (Peachey, 1995), the overwhelming majority of Đông Hồ paintings are sold in winter, right before Tết. In addition to traditional woodblock prints, a few contemporary Vietnamese printmakers have employed Western printmaking techniques, like linoblock printing, on dó paper (Figure 7h).

True paintings on dó and other papers can still be found outside of Đông Hồ Village. Among the Dao Tiền people of Đà Bắc District, painting has historically been an important

Figure 8. Dao Tiền paintings, depicting legendary emperors. From an archive belonging to a Dao Tiền family living in Sưng Village, Đà Bắc District. Photographed by J. O., November 4, 2022.

method for depicting histories, stories, and legends, especially of ancient royalty. These are typically brightly colored, prominently featuring a bust or full-body portrait of a king or emperor, and adorned with clouds, animals, and/or courtesans (Figure 8). Although the authors witnessed several beautiful examples of Dao Tiền paintings in Sưng Village (Figure 9), they were all decades old, and often cracking, torn, or fragmenting, leading us to speculate that Dao Tiền icon painting traditions may now unfortunately be either severely endangered or extinct.

2.5.2 Worship

As with many kinds of bamboo paper in China (McClure, 1986), dó paper has long played major roles in Vietnamese worship, ceremonies, and celebrations—often through burning, including as votive paper, as packaging for fireworks, and in incense (Vũ, 2008). As with the purchase and gifting of Đông Hồ paintings during holidays like Tết, dó paper burning commemorates joyous or auspicious occasions. One of the largest celebrations still employing handmade dó today are the Dao Tiền coming-of-age ceremonies, which take place when boys turn 10 years old. During these ceremonies, shamans chant and burn many sheets of handmade dó paper to summon spirits that protect the boy as he becomes a man (James Ojascastro, personal communication, November 4, 2022).

The burning of dó paper is also associated with more solemn occasions, including funerals, ceremonies for venerating the ancestors, and rituals for cleansing, healing, and purifying. For example, the first two authors witnessed a Dao Tiền ceremony one evening conducted by a local shaman to dispel the evil spirits causing his child's illness. Before the ceremony, sheets of dó were cut into rectangles and embossed with a wooden stamp (Figure 9a, b), to create

Figure 9. Dao Tiền rituals using dó paper. a) Wooden stamper used for embossing patterns into dó paper. b) Detail of the stamping end of the stamper, showing 18 circle motifs in a 6 × 3 arrangement. c) Pile of embossed dó paper "money" being burned as part of a healing ritual in Sưng Village, Đà Bắc District. d) Shaman reading from a book used in Dao Tiền rituals. e) Detail of a shaman's ritual book, written in the Iu Mien language using Chinese characters. f) Detail of a paper spirit, created by drawing a spirit icon on a small rectangle of dó paper and then cutting the sheet into a roughly humanoid shape. g) Spirits cut from dó paper and tacked above a window.

"money" (Figure 9c). Then an altar was prepared with incense and offerings of food and positioned under a lamp just outside the door of the shaman's house. The ceremony began with one of the ill child's brothers burning a pile of the "money" at their doorstep while the shaman chanted from a prayer book (also made from dó paper and written in the Iu Mien language using Chinese characters; Figure 9d, e). Another brother sat before the altar, chanting alongside his father, and clapping two pieces of wood at regular intervals. The ceremony concluded after all the votive paper burned to ash (James Ojascastro, personal communication, November 4, 2022).

Dó paper can also be employed in worship and ritual through non-incendiary ways. Several different ethnic groups across Việt Nam invoke the powers of spirits simply by drawing on handmade paper (Figure 9f) and/or cutting the sheets into humanoid shapes (practices that are analogous to those of the Hñähñu in central Mexico, who make amate sheets and cut them into ornate figurines of spirits; León & Ojascastro, 2024; Peters, et al., 1987; von Hagen, 1943). Once manifested by pen or blade, the Vietnamese paper spirit is tacked above doorways around the house to confer protection to the family inhabiting within (Figure 9g). Such traditions seem to vary both materially and artistically across ethnic groups. Although Dao Tiền spirit icons are made from dó paper, Hmong communities just a few dozen kilometers west instead use a handmade paper made from a bamboo (*Maclurochloa tonkinensis* H.N.Nguyễn & V.T.Trần; Nguyễn Hoàng Nghĩa, personal communication, January 17, 2024), which they incise with geometric patterns before pinning around the house (Nguyễn, 2023). Despite these regional variations in worship and ritual, the spirituality associated with paper across Việt Nam is unmistakable and pervasive.

Today, machine-made printed papers have begun to displace handmade dó paper as a medium for worship and ritual. Interestingly, this displacement was only apparent to the authors in urban and peri-urban areas, and in cases where the paper was intended to be

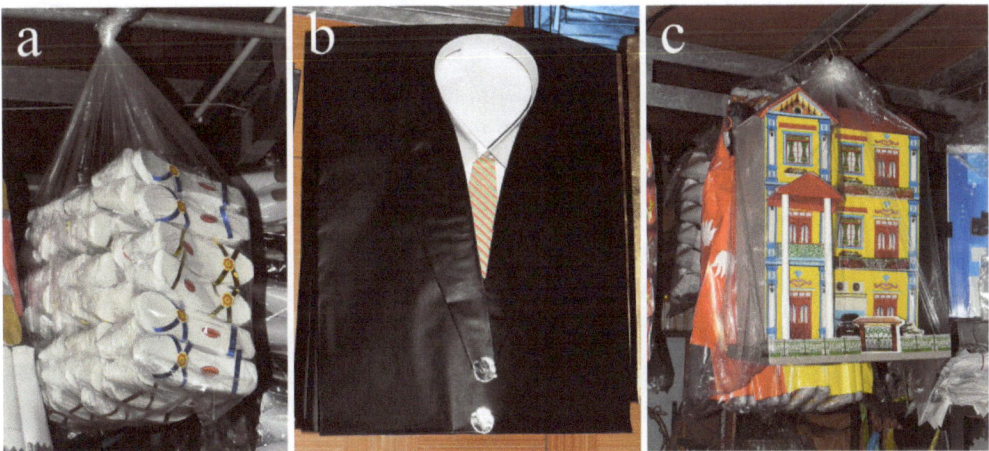

Figure 10. Contemporary votive paper, made by machine from wood pulp, printed, and assembled into three-dimensional shapes. a) Sandals. b) Suit. c) House. Photographed by J.O. in Hà Nội, August 17, 2019.

burned. In Hà Nội, many boutiques now sell three-dimensional, printed, mass-produced, Chinese-made, wood-pulp paper facsimiles of luxury items like suits, watches, houses, and $100 USD bills designed to be burned in lieu of handmade dó paper during Tết, weddings, and other celebrations (Figure 10). Although these machine-made votive paper products are now ubiquitous in cities across Việt Nam, the encroachment of wood-pulp paper for worship does not yet appear to have displaced the usage of handmade paper for household spiritual protection in rural Dao Tiền villages (though it already has in some Hmong villages; Trần Hồng Nhung, personal communication, February 5, 2023). Mechanisms supporting the survival of this tradition in rural areas could include greater accessibility of handmade paper in rural areas, stronger associations between spirits and handmade paper, or a combination of these influences.

One clue supporting the strength of the connection between spirits and handmade paper can be gleaned from the puzzling present state of the Dao Tiền paper economy. In Đà Bắc District, where many Dao Tiền people live, no paper has been made by hand since about 1980. Consequently, shamans must import dó paper from the Kinh papermakers in Phong Khê, which in turn was made from bark Dao Tiền harvesters stripped, dried, and baled months or years prior (Triệu Văn Thanh, personal communication, January 5, 2019). Fortunately, despite a 40-year hiatus, efforts by the second author (T.H.N.) are underway to revive dó papermaking in Đà Bắc; this is described in greater detail in the conclusion section of this monograph.

2.5.3 Royal Edicts

From the mid-17th century until 1944, the Lại family of papermakers were the exclusive manufacturers and suppliers of high-quality dó paper to the lords and emperors of northern Việt Nam. These so-called "royal" (Vietnamese: ***sắc phong***) papers were usually large rectangles that were coated with a sizing made from buffalo skin, colored uniformly with a yellow vegetable-based dye, and decorated with ornate dragons using gold or silver ink before being sent to the ruling class to write decrees and edicts (Hà, 2016; Figure 11a, b). The sources of the yellow dye varied, and they included rhizomes of turmeric (Vietnamese: ***nghệ***; *Curcuma longa* L.), fruits of gardenia (Vietnamese: ***dành dành***; *Gardenia jasminoides* J.Ellis), and/or flowers of pagodatree (Vietnamese: ***hòe***; *Styphnolobium japonicum* [L.] Schott). This last species is in current use by Vietnamese paper conservators to restore the color of old, faded sắc phong artifacts, of which the oldest extant example dates to 1604 (Hà, 2016).

Following the 1945 abdication of Bảo Đại, the last emperor of Việt Nam, there was no more Vietnamese royalty, and so the royal papermaker at the time, Lại Phú Bàn of Bưởi Village, the 17th-generation of papermakers in his family, stopped making sắc phong paper. By this time however, the Lại family had lost knowledge of sheet formation, and Mr. Phú Bàn made sắc phong paper instead by drawing dragons on dó paper he purchased from papermakers in Yên Bái (Trần Hồng Nhung, personal communication, February 5, 2023). Mr. Phú

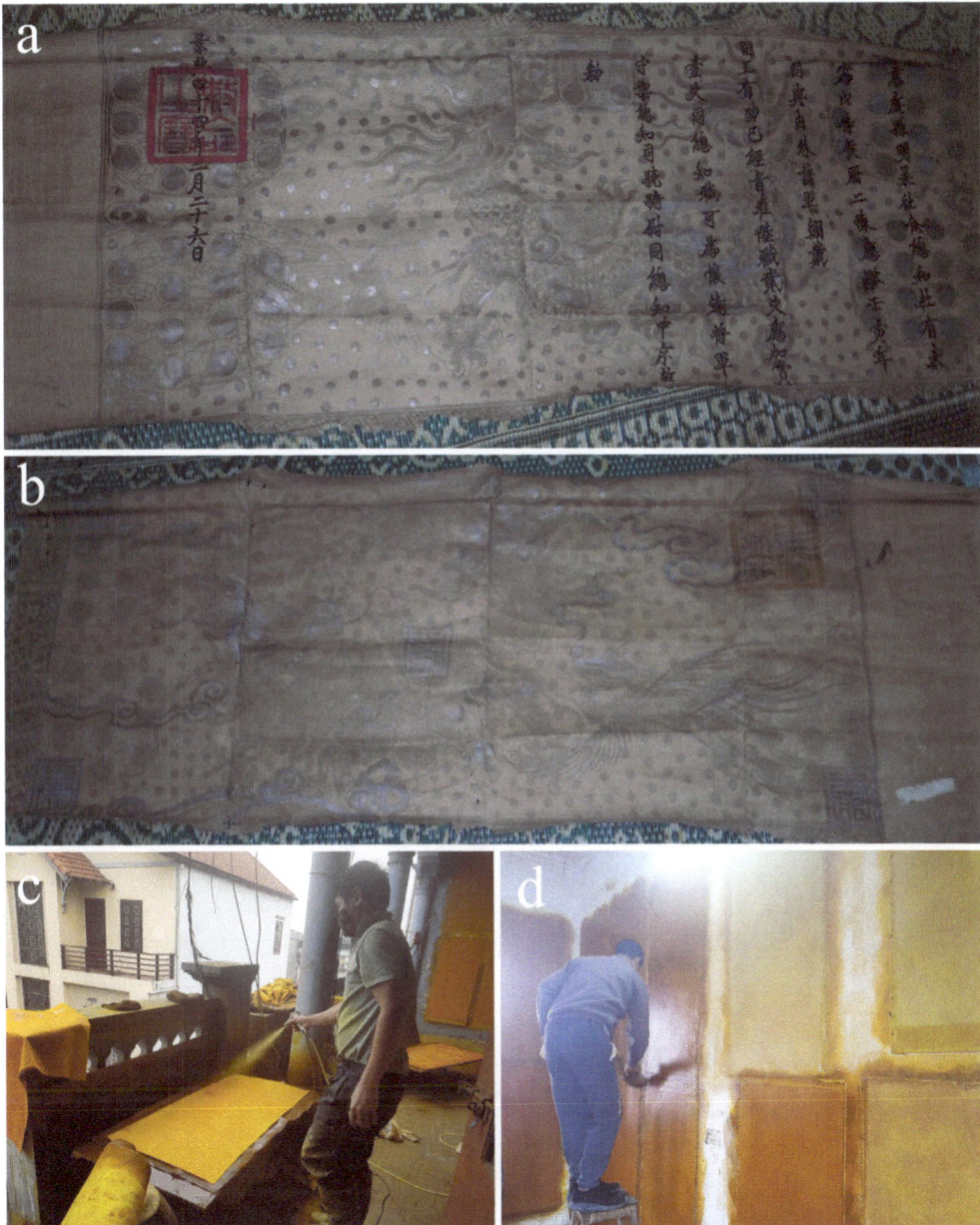

Figure 11. Examples of historical and contemporary sắc phong paper. a) Obverse side of an official order, dated 20 February 1783, issued by Vietnamese Emperor Lê Hiển Tông 黎顯宗 (1717–1786; reigned 1740–1786) to honor a military general; translation by Dr. Wen-Hsi Kuo. b) Reverse side of official order. c) Modern process of making sắc phong paper from dó paper today: papermaker Phạm Văn Tâm uses an airbrush to apply yellow dye to a large (60 x 120 cm) rectangle of dó paper. d) After dyeing, Mr. Tâm dries the still-wet sheet on a concrete wall. Photos a, b by Nguyễn Công Hoàng; c, d by Trần Hồng Nhung.

Bàn continued to be solicited until his death in 2006 for repairs to old sắc phong documents and artifacts made by him and his family decades or centuries prior.

Today, sắc phong paper is made by Phạm Văn Tâm in Bắc Ninh, who uses food-grade yellow coloring, applied either by brush or airbrush (Figure 11c, d), to dye large sheets of dó paper (which he also makes). Although Việt Nam is no longer a monarchy, both the incumbent government and royal descendants still purchase sắc phong paper for use as certificates and official documents.

2.5.4 Gilding

Koretsky (2003) mentions dó paper being used as a substrate for beating and depositing gold leaf, but it is not known if Vietnamese gilders still use dó for this purpose today. Usage of handmade paper in gold beating was widespread across mainland East and Southeast Asia, but the fibers employed for making this specialized paper varied following the local papermaking tradition: for example, Chinese and Burmese goldbeaters used bamboo paper, because bamboo was the chief raw material used in hand papermaking traditions there (Koretsky & Koretsky, 1991; McClure, 1986).

2.5.5 Origami

In the 1950s, a modest though prolific paper artist named Akira Yoshizawa was invited to exhibit his origami pieces at a museum in Holland. Yoshizawa's exhibition, surpassed 4 decades later by an even bigger show at the Louvre, thrust origami onto the global stage, transforming it from a Japanese craft to a global art (Engel, 1989). The world took note, and origami neophytes outside of Japan quickly and zealously embraced paperfolding—experimenting, creating, and collaborating along the way. By the 21st century, some kinds of origami had become so intricate that origami artists needed to tailor the structural demands of so-called "super-complex" designs to specific kinds of paper capable of withstanding the abuse of hundreds or even thousands of folds. While origamists in the West and Japan had easy access to countless specialty papers, many talented artists in low- or middle-income countries did not have this luxury. Constrained by accessibility challenges, one young folder in Hà Nội found a solution—practically in his backyard.

Việt Nam Origami Group (VOG) was founded in 2005 by just a few young artists in Hà Nội, most of whom were still in high school or college. At the time, few kinds of suitable paper were available in Việt Nam to fold complex designs; the paper of choice then was a Chinese-manufactured, textured, crisp, machine-made paper called pearl crumpled paper. But pearl crumpled paper was not without drawbacks: it became brittle if folded excessively, and it was only available in 10 or 12 colors. For want of more durable and customizable papers, some Vietnamese origamists began experimenting with locally available handmade papers.

The use of handmade paper for origami, particularly super-complex origami, was not without precedent. While there are exceptions, industrial wood-pulp papers generally have shorter and more brittle fibers than handmade papers due to the harsher physical and chemical processing involved in manufacturing the former; consequently, handmade papers tend to be stronger and age better than wood-pulp papers, and so many contemporary origami artists pay premiums for handmade specialty papers to fold with. Indeed, Japanese artists long used **washi** (Japanese handmade paper) sheet-formed from cooked and beaten *kōzō* (*Broussonetia × kazinoki* Siebold) fibers for folding, and now, origamists around the world continue to use it for super-complex designs. In addition, artists like Robert Lang and David Gachepapier have co-opted other handmade papers with no history of use in origami, like Philippine abaca, Mexican amate, and Nepalese lokta to suit their folding needs (Gachepapier & Ševerova, 2019; León, 2023). So, it should come as no surprise that when Nguyễn Hùng Cường, one of the founding members of VOG, began posting his art folded from dó paper on social media, the origami world took note, and paper suppliers in France and the United States started to buy dó from vendors in Hà Nội and directly from papermakers in Phong Khê.

Like the Đông Hồ printmakers, Vietnamese origami artists must treat their dó first, because it is too soft and insufficiently crisp to fold untreated. To do this, Mr. Cường smooths a sheet of dó on glass, brushes a watery solution of white polyvinylacetate (PVA) glue (Vietnamese: **keo**) onto it, and leaves it to dry almost completely. When the sheet is still slightly damp, he peels it carefully off the glass and hangs it to dry completely. The treated sheet is stiffer and can be folded and shaped thenceforth. Moreover, color can be tailored easily by mixing a few drops of acrylic paint in with the PVA solution before application. By demonstrating the versatility and suitability of dó for new artistic purposes, Mr. Cường and Vietnam Origami Group not only broadened the corpus of origami knowledge, but also provided a way for paper artists around the world to financially support indigenous papermakers and help keep their traditions alive.

2.6 Current Status

Although dó is still the predominant paper made by hand today in Việt Nam by far, that is not at all to say its future is guaranteed. Restrictive government policies, industrialization, and economic transitioning over the latter half of the 20th century have made it nearly impossible for Vietnamese paper artisans to make a living using traditional methods. Although war, first with France and then with the United States, certainly disrupted papermaking industries at times, documentation of this between the mid-1950s through the end of the 1970s are scarce to nonexistent. On the contrary, artisans at Đông Hồ reported that papermakers, painters, and printmakers across northern Việt Nam ramped up production during the French and American wars to produce flyers, posters, newspapers, and other propaganda; the artisans in Dương Ổ even supplied paper used in the manufacture of army batteries (Fanchette & Stedman, 2009).

Following Việt Nam's reunification in 1975, a combination of urbanization and liberalizing economic reforms (Vietnamese: *Đổi Mới*) caused Hà Nội to absorb Yên Thái and nearby craft villages, extinguishing their hand papermaking industries by the 1980s and replacing them with cafés and other small businesses. As urban growth continued, the government enforced a 1994 law prohibiting the detonation of fireworks in Hà Nội to mitigate fire risk, especially during holidays like Tết; this legislation pushed even more hand papermakers towards insolvency, because most of the gunpowder envelopes in firecrackers were made of low-quality dó paper supplied by papermakers in in Dương Ổ (Fanchette, 2016). Moreover, as the Cold War ended, Western nations began lifting their sanctions and embargos with Việt Nam, further empowering factory industry at the expense artisanal trades. Consequently, dozens of the remaining dó-papermaking families in Bắc Ninh invested in massive pulping and recycling machines to manufacture mass-produced paper goods like newspaper, toilet paper, and napkins. Those who made this transition often became extremely wealthy, and many of the streets of Phong Khê are lined with walled, multi-storey mansions built by "toilet paper barons." Meanwhile, the small guilds of papermaking families who still maintain their manual tradition struggle to sell their more expensive, handmade paper to a market whose demand has evaporated almost completely—now limited to niche artistic and religious uses. Quantification brings the plight of hand papermaking in Việt Nam into sharper focus: as recently as 1980, some 5,000 people in Dương Ổ were involved in dó papermaking; by 2019, this had dwindled to just 15 people spread across three families (Phạm Văn Tầm, personal communication, January 14, 2019). Within these family papermaking industries, most of the workers are employed in fiber processing: in 2008, just five people in Dương Ổ were responsible for sheet formation (Fanchette & Stedman, 2009), and by 2012, only three were left.

3. Dưỡng

Broussonetia papyrifera (L.) L'Héritier ex Vent.
Family Moraceae

3.1 Introduction

Dưỡng is a rapidly growing dioecious suckering tree, 10 to 20 m tall. Its leaves are usually alternate (but sometimes opposite or whorled), serrate, unlobed or trilobed, and pubescent (especially abaxially). Male flower clusters are catkinate, while female inflorescences are globose, maturing after fertilization to yield a red, edible, fleshy syncarp (Figure 12a; Yatskievych, 2013).

For centuries, dưỡng has been used by many mainland East and Southeast Asian cultures for medicine, alimentation, timber, fiber, and even money (Cartwright et al., 2014). Seafaring Austronesians, recognizing the utility of this plant, brought dưỡng with them in their trans-Pacific island migrations to make barkcloth variously called siapo, kapa, or tapa (Peña-Ahumada et al., 2020; Peñalillo et al., 2016). Later, Europeans introduced dưỡng to North America, where it has been cultivated since at least 1812—the year Thomas Jefferson planted several for shade at his Monticello estate (Gary, 2012). In the 2 centuries since, dưỡng has escaped cultivation and become a weedy, thicket-forming invasive across the US Southeast (Richard, 2010; Yatskievych, 2013). Today, dưỡng has a largely cosmopolitan distribution across most tropical and warm-temperate terrestrial ecosystems. Thanks to its ubiquity and utility, many languages have a vernacular name for *Broussonetia papyrifera*, including ***daluang*** (Indonesian), ***saa*** (Thai), ***kajinoki*** (Japanese), and "paper mulberry" (English). Since the vignettes described here span two ethnic groups in Việt Nam, each with their own vernacular names for *B. papyrifera*, we have elected to refer to this species using the name in the Vietnamese language (dưỡng) for consistency.

The utility, commonness, broad distribution, and climatic tolerance of dưỡng grant it a unique cross-cultural status in hand papermaking traditions, and the manufacture of paper, paper-like materials, and barkcloth from its inner bark fibers plays an integral role in many Asian and Oceanian nations, including Việt Nam. Yet despite its versatility and usefulness

Figure 12. Mường process of making dướng paper in Suối Cỏ Village, Lương Sơn District, Hòa Bình Province. a) Leaves and fruits of *Broussonetia papyrifera*, August 2019, Hà Nội, Việt Nam. b) Cutting dướng trunks and branches, harvested from forests surrounding Suối Cỏ, to approximately 1-m lengths. c) Boiling trunks and branches to ensure the bark peels off the wood easily. d) Nguyễn Văn Chúc peeling dướng bark off the wood following boiling. e) Mr. Chúc scraping the green bark from the white bark using a sharp knife. In Suối Cỏ, both green bark and white bark are used to make paper products. f) Cooking white bark in lime. g) After cooking, the bark is rinsed thoroughly and beaten by hand, using mallets carved from guava wood. h) After manual beating, the fibers are further processed in a naginata beater. i) Nguyễn Thị Hậu demonstrating sheet formation using a khung seo and liêm seo. j) Mrs. Hậu couching a sheet of dướng paper. k) Expelling of excess water from a post using a screw press. l) Mrs. Hậu peeling dướng sheets in the post apart by hand. m) Drying dướng sheets in the sun.

elsewhere, unambiguous historical records of dướng specifically being used for papermaking in Việt Nam are scarce, due partly to Western failures to distinguish between dó and dướng (Bouvier, 1940; Hunter, 1947), and partly to what must be a substantial Vietnamese preference in using dó over dướng for the manufacture of paper. French officials traveled to Japan in the early 20th century to document how the species was harvested to make kōzō paper (Claverie, 1904), suggesting that dướng was not known to them as comparably favorable, profitable, and exploitable to dó in Indochina. This French research neither inspired any notable increase in dướng usage for paper in Việt Nam, nor dislodged the primacy of dó as the chief raw material for handmade paper in the Hồng River Valley. Indeed, in the decades since French occupation, Vietnamese papermaking traditions using solely dướng disappeared almost entirely (although some papermakers in Bắc Ninh still mix up to 20% dướng fiber in certain dó sheets; Trần Hồng Nhung, personal communication, February 6, 2023), with perhaps just two examples still extant: one long practiced by the Nùng ethnic group along the Chinese border, and another recently revived by a Mường village just outside of Hà Nội. These dướng papermaking case studies have benefited from initiatives by the Vietnamese government and social enterprises that train local artisans and help them earn supplemental income by making handmade paper products that can be sold throughout Việt Nam and around the world.

3.1.1 Mường

The Mường, native to the foothills and mountains west of Hà Nội, are the third most populous ethnic group in Việt Nam; their language, also called Mường, is closely related to Vietnamese. Like the Nùng, the Mường have traditions of making paper from dướng (Mường: *ràng*) phloem fibers, but they have been slightly less fortunate: sometime during the war with the United States, the Mường stopped making dướng paper, and their papermaking tradition became extinct. In 2006, the Việt Nam Association of Craft Villages orchestrated a 6-year initiative to restore lost papermaking traditions to the Mường people, designed in part to help new Mường artisans earn supplemental income through the construction and sale of paper and papercrafts. This initiative invited Japanese papermakers to Việt Nam to help train the Mường villagers, who responded by blending Japanese techniques with those practiced in Bắc Ninh for dó, to create a new technique to process dướng fiber into paper. Despite the explicitly economic intentions of this initiative, which ended in 2012, the Mường papermakers struggled to make a living practicing their new trade, and many soon returned to previous sources of income (chiefly farming). However, some Mường papermakers persevered, alternating their time between papermaking and traveling, often to Hà Nội, to make and sell their handicrafts. In 2014, these persevering Mường papermakers partnered with Zó Project, a social enterprise founded by the second author (T.H.N.) of this paper, based in Hà Nội, to help sell their paper handicrafts across Việt Nam and around the world. Zó Project now works with a cooperative of five Mường families, based in Suối Cỏ Village, Hòa Bình

Province, to grow, harvest, and process dưỡng into postcards, prints, posters, notebooks, calendars, fans, lanterns, and earrings.

3.1.2 Nùng

The Nùng people are a Tai-speaking ethnic group native to northern Việt Nam and southern China. Like many of their neighbors, they are diverse—comprising many subgroups, including the Nùng Inh and Nùng An—and they have maintained a long tradition of making paper for various artistic, religious, and utilitarian purposes. However, many Nùng people have abandoned their papermaking heritage in pursuit of better-paying jobs, often elsewhere in Việt Nam, and only a few Nùng villages in Cao Bằng still make paper. In response to this decline, in 2012–2013, the Department of Labor, War Invalids, and Social Affairs of Cao Bằng Province gave 10 million VND to each of seven poor Nùng households in Lũng Quang Village, Thông Nông Township, Hà Quảng District to build furnaces and vats for papermaking (Tuấn, 2018). Sixty kilometers east, in Rìa Trên Village, Quốc Dân Commune, Nùng artisans make paper for local use as well as for sale to visiting foreigners who patronize nearby homestays (James Ojascastro, personal communication, October 27, 2022). In this underdeveloped part of Việt Nam, both government and tourism have helped Nùng artisans continue preserving their heritage through papermaking and to earn money in a mountainous region where farming is difficult, infrastructure is lacking, and opportunities for economic advancement are scarce.

3.2 Fiber Harvesting

Since the Mường and Nùng process dưỡng fiber somewhat differently in their respective papermaking traditions, we describe both fiber harvesting here, and papermaking in the subsequent subsection, grouped by ethnic group.

3.2.1 Mường Fiber Harvesting

Since dưỡng is a weedy, fast-growing tree tolerant of human disturbance, it can be either foraged or cultivated to obtain the requisite phloem fiber necessary for making paper, and it is common to see shifts in management methods over time and across cultures. Such is the case, for example, in the United States, where dưỡng has escaped cultivation and become a troublesome invasive species. Today, paper mulberry is so common across the US Southeast that papermakers living there can harvest it opportunistically without needing to cultivate it (Fulling, 1956; Richard, 2010).

In the contemporary revival of Mường papermaking, fiber harvesters have alternated between cultivating and foraging dưỡng trees depending on their local availability. Some trees are cultivated in backyard gardens and pruned of their top and lateral branches to encourage the main trunk to grow thick and straight; the pruned-off material is commonly used as pig feed. When backyard trees are not available for harvest, either because they have been harvested too recently, or because there are simply not enough trees for a desired batch of paper, the Mường papermakers in Suối Cỏ Village go to the nearby town of Lương Sơn to forage from the dướng growing there.

Recently, collaboration between the Mường papermaking cooperative and Zó Project has yielded a third option—growing and maintaining dướng in the nearby forest. This experiment began in 2016, when dướng was planted in a hillside forest adjacent to Suối Cỏ. The trees take 2 years to achieve a harvestable size after planting, and they were felled in December 2018. Due to the longer time needed to grow dướng trees under the forest canopy, it is unclear if these trees will regenerate and yield usable fiber for the Mường cooperative in the future.

Mường papermakers procure their fiber by using machetes to cut dướng trees down to stumps; this is preferentially done from January through April, when dướng is best able to regenerate. They then cut off any side branches, tie the felled trunks into shorter bundles (Figure 12b), and tip the bundles at an angle to drain excess latex before transporting the bundles over their shoulders back to the fiber processing and papermaking area in Suối Cỏ: the driveway of Nguyễn Văn Chúc and his wife, Nguyễn Thị Hậu. Each dướng tree yields roughly 30 sheets of paper with dimensions 40 × 60 cm (Nguyễn Văn Chúc, personal communication, January 2019).

Papermakers in Japan and the United States often find it difficult to remove bark and phloem from the wood of *Broussonetia* species when fresh. In both Japan and the United States, papermakers rectify this by steaming bundles of branches, which may take anywhere from 10 or 15 min (Barrett, 1983; Nicholas Cladis, personal communication, November 27, 2021) to 2 hr (Aimee Lee, personal communication, March 3, 2023), depending on the size of the branch and the type of *Broussonetia* being processed. Mường artisans face the same challenge with local dướng, but they overcome this difficulty differently. After cutting dướng to about 1-m lengths, the Mường papermakers arrange the trunk sections vertically in a large cauldron, next adding 500 g of lime and enough water to fill the cauldron. Once the lime is fully dissolved, the Mường start a fire under the cauldron and boil the branches in the limewater for 2 or 3 hr (Figure 12c). Like with steaming (Barrett, 1983), the boiling process makes the *Broussonetia* bark shrink slightly on the branch, a visual indication that the bark and phloem are now soft and can be easily peeled from the wood (Figure 12d).

3.2.2 Nùng Fiber Harvesting

Like with the Mường, a shift towards dướng cultivation also happened among Nùng papermakers. Decades ago, dướng (Nùng: *may sla* or *năng sla*) was harvested wild from forests across northern Cao Bằng Province. But following government bans on forest usage and resource extraction, the Nùng adapted by planting dướng seeds—collected from forest trees—

in their gardens and fields; on average, each family maintains about 0.5 ha of dướng trees in cultivation for papermaking (Nông, 2015). Dướng trees are even planted along the road into Lũng Quang Village (Chiến, 2020) and Rìa Trên Village (James Ojascastro, personal communication, October 27, 2022).

Nùng harvesters cut branches from these cultivated dướng during the months of February, March, June, and July (Chiến, 2020; Nông, 2015), in contrast to the late fall harvest practiced in Japan (Barrett, 1983; Nicholas Cladis, personal communication, November 5, 2021). Across papermaking villages in Cao Bằng, dướng trees grow very rapidly, and any given tree growing there could be coppiced as frequently as every year (James Ojascastro, personal communication, October 27, 2022). Bark is removed manually without steaming or boiling, and either dried for long-term storage or processed immediately. If immediately, Nùng artisans soak bark for 10 min in boiling water. If preparing dried bark, they will rehydrate it for 2 or 3 hr before cooking and beating it.

3.3 Mường Papermaking

3.3.1 Fiber Processing

Mường papermakers in Suối Cỏ make sheets of two different qualities, depending on which bark tissues are retained. After the first boiling (to remove the bark from the wood), the bark is washed and scraped (Figure 12e), to separate the innermost bark layer ("white bark"; Vietnamese: *vỏ trắng*) from the green bark (Vietnamese: *vỏ xanh*) and black bark (Vietnamese: *vỏ đen*) layers atop it. The black bark, which largely flakes off of the green bark, is discarded, and the remaining green and white bark layers are retained and then boiled separately, following different recipes. The green bark, which is weaker and less fibrous, is boiled for about 12 hr in limewater, while the tougher and more fibrous white bark is boiled around 18 hr (Figure 12f). After the second boiling, both green bark and white bark are rinsed with fresh water several times until all the lime is washed out. Led by Mr. Nguyễn Văn Chúc, the barks (both green and white) are then beaten separately on wooden boards with mallets carved from *ổi* (guava; *Psidium guajava* L.) wood (Figure 12g). To remove any remaining knots or clumps in the pulp, both green and inner dướng bark are processed further (and separately) in a naginata beater—as is used in Japan with kōzō fiber—each for about 10 min (Figure 12h). Once fully beaten, the pulped dướng inner bark is picked over for 1 or 2 days to remove any remaining knots, toughened or lignified fiber, and flecks of green bark; the lower-quality green bark pulp is not given the same degree of scrutiny. If paper with leaf inclusions or notebook paper will be made, bleach will be added to the batch of pulped inner bark; the now-whitened fibers are then rinsed well to flush out the bleach. After beating and picking, both green and white barks are ready for sheet formation.

3.3.2 Formation Aid

Mường papermakers use a synthetic formation aid, probably polyethylene oxide.

3.3.3 Sheet Formation and Drying

In Suối Cỏ, Mường artisans make paper year-round. After Nguyễn Văn Chúc and neighbors in the cooperative have finished cooking and beating the dướng bark, Mr. Chúc's wife Nguyễn Thị Hậu takes over with sheet formation. After adding dướng pulp and formation aid to a bể seo (vat) filled with water, Mrs. Hậu uses a bamboo rod to whisk the ingredients until the fibers are uniformly dispersed in the bể seo; unlike in nagashizuki, no **mazé** (comb-like agitator) is used for additional or supplemental fiber whisking. Once the pulp is evenly distributed and the proper viscosity of the fiber suspension is reached, Mrs. Hậu pulls sheets from the bể seo using a seo technique identical to that used by the dó papermakers in Bắc Ninh (Figure 12i). She stacks the dướng sheets in a post, sometimes interleaving threads between the sheets (especially if the sheets are thin or have decorative inclusions in them) at one corner to assist with separation following pressing (Figure 12j). Once the desired number of sheets are made, Mrs. Hậu carefully adds a cloth to the top of the completed post and the post is placed in a screw press (Figure 12k), which is turned incrementally every few hours to gradually expel excess water from the post (James Ojascastro, personal communication, January 7, 2019).

After 12 hr or so of gradual pressing, the post is taken out of the press and the cover cloth is removed. One by one, Mrs. Hậu gingerly peels each sheet off the post (Figure 12l), flipping each over to brush the underside with a soft-bristle brush to reattach any fibers that were raised when peeling the sheet away from the pressed post. Any threads that were interleaved in the post to assist in sheet separation are also removed, one by one, as each sheet is peeled off; the threads are then re-used for subsequent posts. The now-liberated dướng sheets are placed on drying racks in the sun (Figure 12m); each rack can hold eight sheets (two stacks, each four sheets deep).

3.4 Nùng Papermaking

3.4.1 Fiber Processing

Overall, dướng fiber processing among the Nùng is very similar to that of the Mường, but with differences in which bark tissues are processed, the quantity of the ingredients used, and the timing of each step of processing. Among the Nùng, freshly peeled dướng bark is first scraped to remove the cortex (green bark plus black bark) to isolate the phloem (white bark); the former is discarded, and the latter is retained and soaked in limewater in a stone basin for 12 hr (Figure 13a). The phloem, now softened, is then boiled for 3 hr (2 hr if the fiber is from

Figure 13. Nùng process of making dướng paper. a) Basin with lime used to chemically separate dướng phloem fibers. b) Cooked dướng fibers at different stages of beating. c) Nùng fiber beating setup, consisting of a base and mallet made of nghiến (*Burretiodendron hsienmu*) wood. d) Leaf and stem of the khổ háo (*Byttneria aspera*) vine, whose bark is immersed in water to obtain formation aid. e) Cloth bag of khổ háo bark mucilage being strained directly into a large, 300-year-old bể seo made from a hollowed-out nghiến tree. f) Sheet formation, using a phử and chả phử. g) Phử in place on chả phử, with bamboo scraper at top right. h) Method of making phử, where a wooden loom is used to weave báng fibers, weighted by small stones, around individual mảy tàn bamboo splints. i) Aligning a bamboo slat with drawn lines on the phử to form the short edges of newly formed sheets by scraping off excess pulp near the edge of the phử. j) Rocks affixed to wire loops, hung from a wooden lever and used to press wet posts of dướng papers. k) Peeling sheets from a pressed post and l) brushing these on a concrete wall to dry. m) Detail of a Nùng drying brush, fashioned from a mass-produced plastic broom head with plastic bristles. n) Larger dướng sheets drying on wooden drying boards. o) Display case showing Nùng dướng paper products, including notebooks, fans, and origami.

a young tree) in enough limewater to submerge the bark, with 3 kg of lime added for every 10 kg of dướng bark being boiled (James Ojascastro, personal communication, October 27, 2022). After cooking, the fiber is either rinsed briefly and soaked in water for 2 days, or, alternatively, washed under a running tap for 12 hr. After this point, men place clumps of dướng phloem on a slab of **nghiến** (*Burretiodendron hsienmu* W.Y.Chun & F.C.How) wood and beat them thoroughly (and entirely) by hand, using nghiến-wood mallets (Figure 13b, c). Following beating, the resulting dướng pulp is then placed in a bể seo (which also may be made from the hollowed-out trunk of a large nghiến tree) and suspended in water in preparation for seo sheet formation (Tuấn, 2018).

3.4.2 Formation Aid

While few details have been documented previously about formation aids used by Nùng artisans for dướng paper, Tuấn (2018) reports that it is extracted from a vine called "**dây trơn**"; however, the first author (J.O.) reports a different name (Nùng: **khổ háo**). J.O. sent photographs of this khổ háo vine (Figure 13d) to Vietnamese botanist Thanh Sơn Hoàng, who identified it as *Byttneria aspera* Colebr. ex Wall. (Vietnamese: **bích nữ nhọn** or **trôm leo**), a liana belonging to the family Malvaceae.

To prepare formation aid from khổ háo, Nùng papermakers first strip bark from the khổ háo vine. The bark strips are then soaked overnight in water, which liberates and disperses a thick mucilage that is then strained through a cloth into the bể seo (Figure 13e). The Nùng report that khổ háo bark can be reused, and formation aid can be extracted from the same bark strips up to six times. Phrased another way, each batch of bark contains enough formation aid to form a total of 200 sheets of dướng paper (James Ojascastro, personal communication, October 27, 2022).

3.4.3 Sheet Formation and Drying

The Nùng use seo for making paper from dướng fiber (Figure 13f), using a bamboo screen (Nùng: **phử**) supported from underneath by a wooden frame (Nùng: **chả phử**; Figure 13g). However, the construction of these tools is different than the liềm seo and khung seo used in dó (and Mường dướng) papermaking. Again, perhaps the greatest similarities are between the bamboo screens, which are essentially identical in structure and method of construction but differ primarily in which raw materials are used. In contrast to liềm seo—which is composed of tre splints woven together with monofilament fishing line—the phử is constructed with splints carefully cut from mōsō bamboo (Nùng: **mảy tàn**; Vietnamese: **trúc sào**; *Phyllostachys edulis* [Carrière] J.Houz.) culms and woven together (Figure 13h) using fibers obtained from the leaves of sugar palm (Vietnamese: **báng**; *Arenga pinnata* [Wurmb] Merr.). Finally, unlike the unmarked liềm seo, the phử is drawn on with permanent marker with lines parallel to the báng-fiber chain lines, but to contextualize the purpose of these markings, we must first describe the structure of the chả phử.

In contrast to the bamboo screens, more notable differences exist between the khung seo and its Nùng counterpart, the chả phử. Although both khung seo and chả phử are similar materially (both made from dổi wood), they are quite different structurally; unlike the two-piece khung seo, the Nùng chả phử is a single, unhinged frame that supports the phử from the bottom. Consequently, since there is no second frame placed on top of the phử, demarcation of the edge of newly formed sheets is done by hand with visual cues. Using black lines drawn on the phử as a guide, the papermaker scrapes excess fiber off the phử and into the bể seo with a broad, blunt, bamboo tool (Figure 13i) before couching the wet pulp that remains on the screen. By following these margin lines drawn directly on the bamboo splints of the phử, many sheets of a standardized size can be made.

Both Nùng women and men seem to be involved in seo, although most of those interviewed seem to be women (Chiến, 2020; Nông, 2015; James Ojascastro, personal communication, October 27, 2022; Tuấn, 2018). About 60 sheets (each about 34 × 60 cm) are couched per post, which is then pressed using a lever weighted with stones to expel excess water (James Ojascastro, personal communication, October 27, 2022; Tuấn, 2018; Figure 13j). After pressing, the layers of the post are peeled apart one by one (Figure 13k), and each sheet is then brushed on concrete walls (Figure 13l, m) or drying boards (Figure 13n) to dry outside (James Ojascastro, personal communication, October 27, 2022)—although at least one source reports that the Nùng have used heated metal plates to dry paper too (Chiến, 2020). Once dry, the paper is sorted into packs of 10 sheets each, ready for sale (Nông, 2015; Tuấn, 2018).

Although dướng fiber is only harvested in the springtime, the Nùng make paper year-round, as a reliable financial supplement to livelihoods primarily focused on farming and animal husbandry. From plant to paper requires a processing time of about 5 days, and 30 or 40 kg of bark yield 400–800 sheets of paper (Nông, 2015; Tuấn, 2018). A batch of 800 sheets sells at market for about 1 million VND (about $46 USD), and two batches of paper can be made per day (Nông, 2015).

3.5 Uses

How dướng paper is used depends on who makes it. Dướng paper made by the Nùng people tends to be consumed locally for traditional uses, including for spiritual practices, packaging, and for art and handicrafts (Figure 13o). Since Nùng dướng paper can withstand the local warm, damp climate for decades and since Cao Bằng is a remote province, handmade paper is still locally prized and machine-made wood-pulp paper has made little headway displacing it (Tuấn, 2018).

However, since the Mường papermaking tradition briefly went extinct, and since Suối Cỏ is much more accessible to the Hà Nội economy, rekindling local interest in and usage of dướng rather than industrially-made paper is more difficult. Instead, most Mường dướng paper is sent to Hà Nội and sold by Zó Project as stationery, jewelry, and home décor to visiting tourists.

3.5.1 Writing

Dướng paper is tough but absorbent, so it is well-suited for brush-based writing and painting. The Nùng use their dướng for writing Confucian texts, which use Chinese characters (Tuấn, 2018), and, more recently, to make notebooks for sale to visitors staying at nearby homestays. The Mường dướng is usually written on by Kinh calligraphers at Zó Project in Hà Nội to make posters and scrolls bearing auspicious blessings for sale to tourists.

3.5.2 Burning

The Nùng still use dướng in ritual burning, mainly as votive paper. Like the Cao Lan people (see the vignette below on **Haupau**), the Nùng emboss their paper with stampers, cut them into banknote-sized rectangles, and burn them on holidays, special occasions, and auspicious dates to venerate ancestors and welcome prosperity for the future (Tuấn, 2018). The Nùng also use dướng for decorating altars and to make sticks of incense (Tuấn, 2018).

The Mường, however, no longer use dướng for ritual burning; machine-made wood-pulp votive papers have already displaced handmade dướng in Mường paper burning ceremonies (James Ojascastro, personal communication, August 17, 2019).

3.5.3 Packaging

The Nùng use their handmade dướng paper as a high-quality wrapping paper or packaging tissue for dishes like sticky rice and cakes. It is used especially during festive occasions where lots of eating occurs, like weddings (Nông, 2015). Dướng is prized as a food-packing material because of its fragrance, ability to keep food fresh, and non-greasy texture.

Due to the cost relative to machine-made wrapping paper and tissue paper, the Mường do not use their dướng for packaging foodstuffs today.

3.5.4 Coloring

Many handmade papers from other countries sold for export, like Nepalese lokta and Thai kōzō, are available in a rainbow of colors. In most cases, exported hand sheets are colored with synthetic dyes, but these colorants are bold, lightfast, sometimes toxic, and not indigenous to any region. Despite this, most cultures have traditions of dyeing with naturally occurring substances, usually for textiles and sometimes also for culinary use. Natural dyes and pigments, with a few notable exceptions—like black walnut and indigo—tend to fade with age and sun exposure and can therefore be difficult to market for export when color stability is desirable.

However, sustainability and cultural literacy are also becoming increasingly important to consumers too. In 2019, rather than adopting a palette of synthetic dyes, Zó Project and the papermakers in Suối Cỏ began co-opting traditional Mường medicinal and culinary plants for dướng paper (Trần, 2022). These plants, which may grow either in Mường home gardens or in the forests surrounding Mường villages, are traditionally used for food, for treating diseases, and for dyeing dishes like sticky rice to celebrate special occasions. At present, four Mường plants have been found suitable for dyeing Mường dướng paper: ***cẩm hồng*** (*Dicliptera tinctoria* [Nees] Kostel.), ***hoàng đằng*** (*Fibraurea tinctoria* Lour.), ***vải thiều*** (lychee; *Litchi chinensis* J.F.Gmel.), and ***củ nâu*** (*Dioscorea cirrhosa,* the same tuber used for dyeing liềm seo bamboo splints).

Cẩm hồng is a perennial herb whose flowers, which may be red, yellow, or purple, are traditionally used to dye sticky rice. However, experiments showed that only the red cẩm hồng flowers can dye paper, yielding an attractive shade of pink. Hoàng đằng is a vine used in traditional Mường medicine. Its roots are a source of a lightfast dye that can turn dướng paper a bright canary yellow. Orange colors can be obtained from two Mường plants. Lychee, though primarily cultivated for its edible fruits, has a colorant in its bark that can be transferred to paper, turning it an earthy orange hue. The tuber of củ nâu is also used to dye dướng orange, but has the advantage of intensifying to a darker, reddish-brown shade over time.

3.6 Current Status

Including both Mường and Nùng ethnic groups, it is likely that only a few dozen to no more than a few hundred people currently practice dướng papermaking in Việt Nam. However, given its occurrence in remote provinces with rugged terrain, it is possible that other ethnic groups still do so (or at least have done so in the recent past), and comprehensive ethnographic surveys may shed more light on the prevalence of this practice.

Surveys in Nùng villages across Cao Bằng Province would not only be a good starting point to refine this estimate, but could also better characterize their harvesting, fiber processing, and sheet-forming techniques beyond what is presented here. So far, nearly all prior documentation on Nùng papermaking has been focused on one hamlet (Lũng Quang) composed of 15 households, all of which participate at least part-time in traditional hand papermaking (Nông, 2015), but other Nùng villages in Cao Bằng Province have papermakers too, presumably also using dướng fiber (Tuấn, 2018).

Among the Mường ethnic group, the only documented papermakers all live in Suối Cỏ Village (population 570), all of whom learned papermaking within the last 15 years. Of 160 households in Suối Cỏ, just five participate in the village's sole papermaking cooperative (Mạnh, 2019).

4. Dó liệt

Wikstroemia indica (L.) C.A.Mey.
Family Thymelaeaceae

4.1 Introduction

Dó liệt is a shrub, 0.5 to 2 m tall, that grows in tropical and semitropical forests across India, southern China, southeast Asia, and western Oceania (Figure 14a). It bears oppositely arranged leaves that may be obovate, elliptic, or lanceolate in shape. Flowers are tetramerous, lacking petals, and bearing instead green sepals fused into a long tube, save for four splayed lobes at the distal end. Following pollination, flowers yield to ellipsoidal red drupes that ripen during the latter half of the year (Wang et al., 2007).

When dó liệt began to be used for textiles and paper is not known. A blanket allegedly made from felted dó liệt (*Wikstroemia viridiflora* Wall. ex Meisn., syn. *W. indica*) fibers made in China during the second half of the 19th century is now in the Royal Botanic Gardens Kew Ethnobotany Collection (Prendergast, 2002), and samples of Chinese dó liệt paper collected by botanist Floyd McClure in the 1920s were pasted in Elaine Koretsky's reprinting of his master's thesis (McClure, 1986). The history of the species' use in Việt Nam is equally nebulous: both colonial-era publications in French (Crevost & Lémarié, 1920; Laroque, 2020; Leandri, 1949; Lecomte et al., 1915) and post-independence publications in English (Peachey, 1995) report *Wikstroemia indica* being used in Vietnamese hand papermaking, but these claims are very likely just misidentifications of dó (*Rhamnoneuron balansae*). Only one unambiguous example of dó liệt papermaking in Việt Nam survives today—on the outskirts of Vinh, in Nghi Phong Commune, Nghi Lộc District, Nghệ An Province—where it has been practiced by at least four consecutive generations of Kinh artisans (Nguyễn Văn Hoá, personal communication, August 14, 2019). As of 2019, just five families in Nghi Phong still make dó liệt paper by hand.

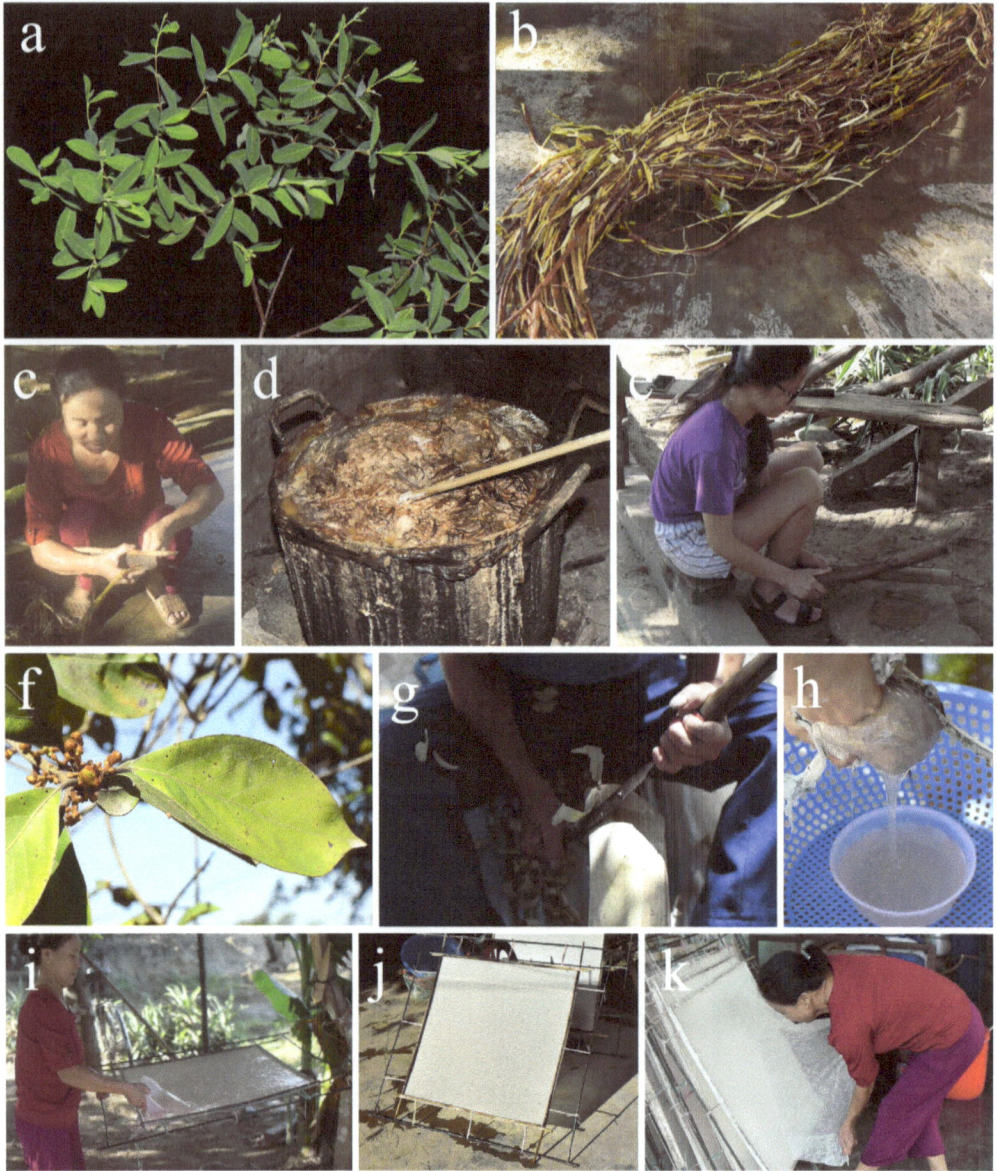

Figure 14. Process of making dó liệt paper in Nghi Lộc District, Nghệ An Province. a) Foliage of *Wikstroemia indica,* whose phloem is the source of fibers for dó liệt paper, Quỳnh Lưu, Nghệ An, Việt Nam. b) Strips of dó liệt bark. c) Vương Thị Loan scraping dó liệt bark to remove the cortex. d) Cooking dó liệt bark in lime water. e) Lê Hồng Kỳ beating cooked dó liệt fibers using guava wood mallets. f) Leaves and flower buds of bìm bìm (*Actinodaphne pilosa*), whose wood, when soaked in water, secretes the mucilaginous formation aid necessary for dó liệt sheet formation. g) Shaving bìm bìm wood for making mucilage. h) Straining bìm bìm wood shavings through mosquito netting to expel a very viscous formation aid. i) Mrs. Loan using a pour mould, consisting of mosquito netting and bamboo stems stretched onto a square rebar frame, and supported on one end by a papermaker and on the opposite end by a hook. A slurry of cooked and beaten dó liệt bark mixed with bìm bìm mucilage and water is poured onto the frame, and the papermaker pivots the frame to uniformly distribute the fibers on the mosquito netting before the mucilage drains from it entirely. j) Dó liệt papermaking frame drying in the sun. k) Mrs. Loan peeling dried dó liệt paper off the frame.

4.2 Fiber Harvesting

Dó liệt stems are harvested wild in Quỳnh Lưu District (19.2°N, 105.6°E), north of Vinh; the majority of this is sold to China for use in traditional medicine as an abortifacient, purgative, and antipyretic. Only a small amount of harvested material is purchased by artisans in Nghệ An for papermaking. Unlike dó, the harvesting technique for dó liệt involves severing the entire stem very close to the ground. Stems are then decorticated and dried for several days, depending on the weather, before being shipped.

4.3 Papermaking

4.3.1 Fiber Processing

Dried bark from Quỳnh Lưu is sent in 35 kg shipments to papermakers in Nghi Phong, who store the bark above ground under the eaves of their backyard sheds until the fibers are ready to be processed in small batches (Figure 14b). Dried bark is rehydrated in water for 1 day; once softened, the outer bark is removed with a sharp knife (Figure 14c). The remaining inner bark is cooked in limewater for 2 days (Figure 14d) and then washed to remove the lime. Fiber beating is done on a hard, flattened stone with cylindrical mallets made of guava wood (Figure 14e). Once uniformly beaten, the dó liệt fibers are chemically bleached, rinsed well, picked clean to remove any remaining impurities, and then mixed in a bucket with formation aid (Ojascastro, 2024).

4.3.2 Formation Aid

Like in Dương Ổ, the Vinh papermakers' formation aid is naturally derived from wood shavings soaked in water. However, in Vinh, papermakers instead use wood shaved from **bìm bìm** (*Actinodaphne pilosa* [Lour.] Merr.; Figure 14f, g), also called **bộp long**, as their formation aid source, which is locally available (one tree even grows in the backyard of dó liệt papermakers Nguyễn Văn Hoá and his wife Vương Thị Loan). Bìm bìm shavings need only about 10 min of soaking in water to yield an especially thick mucilage conducive to their style of sheet formation (Ojascastro, 2024). This mucilage is then strained through cheesecloth or mosquito netting to isolate the formation aid from the wood used to generate it (Figure 14h).

4.3.3 Sheet Formation and Drying

Once the formation aid is added to the aqueous fiber suspension, paper sheets can be formed. The principal tool for dó liệt papermaking in Vinh is a pour mould, which is fashioned from a screen of mosquito netting pulled taut by bamboo stretcher bars laced with cotton or synthetic cord on a frame of steel rebar. To make sheets, the Vinh papermakers first mount the corner of rebar opposite them on a post-mounted hook; then, the slurry is poured on the mosquito netting, the mould is tilted around on the hook to uniformly distribute the fibers on the screen, and the fibers slowly settle into a random, interwoven conformation as excess water drains (Figure 14i); this kind of manipulation, where a papermaker manipulates a mould secured at the opposite end to a fixed point, is reminiscent of webal tteugi (Korean sheet formation), where a papermaker arcs a bamboo screen (bal) and pinewood screen support (bal teul)—secured by a rope on the far end to a suspended post—into a vat filled with slurry immediately below (Lee, 2012). However, since Korean bamboo screens are removable and Korean papermakers couch sheets sequentially on posts (or stacks) of paper, here the similarity ends: the wet sheet of dó liệt is left on the pour mould to dry in the sun (Figure 14j), and a new mould is used to make the next dó liệt sheet. Once completely dry, the Vinh papermakers peel the square dó liệt sheets off their moulds (Figure 14k) and fold them into quarters, ready to be sold (Ojascastro, 2024).

4.4 Uses

Historically, dó liệt was used in much the same way as other Vietnamese handmade papers: writing, painting, calligraphy, and burning. In Jiangxi, China, McClure (1986) reported that during the early 20th century, dó liệt paper was used for making lanterns, and as stuffing for insulating winter garments (McClure, 1986). However, as trade and infrastructure have improved across East and Southeast Asia, almost all the former uses of dó liệt have either gone extinct or have been replaced by other kinds of paper. In the case of Việt Nam, nearly all historical uses of dỏ liệt have now been replaced with dó imported from Dương Ổ; for example, dó liệt paper was once used to wrap around agarwood incense sticks to extend their burn time and enhance their fragrance, but dó paper does this even better and is now used for this purpose (Nguyễn Văn Hoá, personal communication, August 14, 2019). Paper burned for ceremonies when family members pass away have similarly shifted from dó liệt to dó. As of 2019, there is a single major reason dó liệt paper is still made, and that is for wrapping fish (Ojascastro, 2024).

In Vinh, a coastal town with a long beach, seafood plays a major role in the diet and economy of its people. Vinh also has a marked wet season, so fish cannot always be dried in the sun to lengthen their shelf life. The solution is to use dó liệt paper: small rectangles are cut from large sheets and then wrapped in a U-shape around the belly of the fish. Although thin, these dó liệt sheets do an excellent job conserving the freshness of fish before it is cooked. Moreover, when it is time to grill the fish, the dó liệt packaging is not removed, to help retain the fish's shape and juiciness. And finally, the thinness of dó liệt paper functions to allow both fishermen and seafood customers to examine the quality of the fish without having to remove the paper wrapper (Nguyễn Văn Hoá, 2019). Together, these niche qualities and uses have enabled the manufacture of dó liệt paper to persist without displacement by either machine-made papers or other handmade Vietnamese papers (Ojascastro, 2024).

4.5 Current Status

The future of dó liệt papermaking is extremely uncertain and can be attributed to several interrelated factors. One is its specialized utility, now limited to wrapping fish. Another is the lack of demand even within its intended market: the Vinh papermakers speculate that this could be due to overfishing off the coast of Vinh, so there may be fewer fishermen available to buy dó liệt paper than before, and/or an increase in using alternative methods of keeping fish fresh, like ice, plastic-based vacuum packaging, and salting. Additionally, fishing itself is seasonal, and the paper, though it is made year-round, can only be sold from February through July, when fish are plentiful in the region. Finally (and consequently), children in papermaking families are not incentivized to continue making paper, because they cannot make enough money throughout the year to survive doing it. As a result, dó liệt papermaking has declined sharply in modern times; as recently as 2010, 70 families in Nghi Phong still made dó liệt paper, but this has fallen to just five families by 2019 (Nguyễn Văn Hoá, personal communication, August 14, 2019).

5. HAUPAU

Linostoma persimile **Craib**
Family Thymelaeaceae

5.1 Introduction

Haupau is a liana native to northern Southeast Asia and southern China (Figure 15a). Its leaves are small, elliptic, entire, and oppositely arranged on wiry, twining stems (Nevling, 1961). It thrives in damp, hilly regions and grows slowly in the understory, climbing the trunks of tall trees toward the canopy.

Field observations of haupau demonstrating its "strong bark" character and lack of mucilage and latex point to haupau being a member of the Thymelaeaceae. Shortly after observation, the first author (J.O.) sent pictures of haupau to Thymelaeaceae specialist Zachary Rogers, who in turn identified the liana as the species *Linostoma persimile* Craib, a species only known previously from northern Thailand and Myanmar (Zachary Rogers, personal communication, August 29, 2019). However, we note that since the only available dichotomous key for *Linostoma* relies on reproductive characters (Nevling, 1961), and neither the authors nor the papermakers have seen haupau flowers (Dương Văn Quảng, personal communication, August 22, 2019), this species determination may be subject to revision should more information become available. In any case, in this vignette, we present the first record of a hand papermaking tradition from the genus *Linostoma*, today practiced in only one village by three people belonging to the Cao Lan ethnic group. Both fiber harvesting and sheet formation occur in the village of Khe Nghè, in Lục Sơn Commune, Lục Nam District, Bắc Giang Province. For this vignette, we refer to *Linostoma* using the Cao Lan common name "haupau"—partly because the Cao Lan are the only known ethnic group that uses it in papermaking, and partly also because the Kinh common name (Vietnamese: ***dó dây***) is ambiguous and can refer to other species (e.g., *Broussonetia kaempferi* Siebold).

Figure 15. Process of making haupau paper. a) Leaves and stems of the haupau (*Linostoma persimile*) liana. b) Dương Văn Quảng demonstrating how to harvest bark from the haupau liana. c) Dried haupau bark collected from the previous year. d) Leaves and flowers of vạt pạ (*Grewia sessilifolia* Gagnep.), whose inner bark is soaked in water to make formation aid as part of haupau papermaking. e) Mr. Quảng scraping away outer bark from strips of vạt pạ phloem. f) Immersing vạt pạ phloem in water to yield formation aid. g) Pour moulds used in Cao Lan papermaking, made of dẻ (*Castanopsis boisii*) wood. h) Haupau paper drying in the sun. i) Wooden stamp with the Dương family talisman used for embossing haupau paper. j) A Cao Lan book made from haupau paper.

5.2 Fiber Harvesting

Haupau bark harvesting occurs just once or twice each summer in the hilly, closed-canopy subtropical rainforest patches northeast of Khe Nghè. In this village, only three harvesters—who in this case also make the haupau paper—still visit the forest to harvest bark. Their technique resembles that of the dó liệt harvesters: harvesters first select stems of appropriate size (4–5 cm diameter, corresponding to 5–7 years of growth; James Ojascastro, personal communication, November 11, 2022), which are then clipped near the ground, and each severed stem is peeled to remove the bark from the xylem (Figure 15b), the latter of which is discarded in the forest. Decortication also serves to remove the thin cortex, which flakes off as the bark is removed (and is important to flake off anyway due to the presence of tiny, irritating hairs that can cause skin rashes). The inner bark strips are dried and stored until they are ready to be processed. The average annual harvest of 10 kg dried haupau fiber is sufficient to maintain the paper needs of their community.

5.3 Papermaking

5.3.1 Fiber Processing

The origin of the Cao Lan papermaking tradition is unknown to the Cao Lan papermakers we interviewed. The main papermaker today, Dương Văn Quảng (Figure 15b), says he first learned it in 1998 at age 30, after completing his service in the Vietnamese Army. Wanting to preserve Cao Lan customs, Mr. Quảng apprenticed for 2 years under the late Tống Văn Xạch and his wife's elder relatives to become the fourth generation in the Dương family to master haupau papermaking (Bao, 2018). Since the elders' passing, only Mr. Quảng and two of his brothers still make haupau paper today. Mr. Quảng has a son who also knows how to make haupau, but it is not clear if he will carry on the family papermaking tradition (Dương Văn Quảng, personal communication, October 26, 2022).

Haupau paper is typically made in winter, using techniques very similar to those used by papermakers in Vinh for dó liệt paper. Dried fiber (Figure 15c) is rehydrated and softened in a bucket of water for just 1 or 2 hr, and then any persisting outer bark is shaved off with a sharp knife. Next, the inner bark is cooked in soda ash for 3 to 4 hr (shorter if more chemical is added), and washed again; if whiter paper is desired, bark is soaked for another 12 hr in a limewater bath (and subsequently rinsed in fresh water) before this step (Dương Văn Quảng, personal communication, October 26, 2022). After cooking, the remaining inner bark is beaten on a stone with wooden mallets until the fibers separate fully from each other; Mr. Quảng reports that any hard wood can be used for beaters, although the ones he was using when we interviewed him were made from guava wood. The beaten fibers are washed yet again, suspended in water, and picked over to remove dirt, ash, and flecks of outer bark. The suspension is then mixed with formation aid in preparation for sheet formation.

5.3.2 Formation Aid

Khe Nghè papermakers obtain their mucilage from a treelet called *vạt pạ* (Vietnamese: *cẩm quỳ*; *Grewia sessilifolia* Gagnep.; Figure 15d). This is done by clipping vạt pạ stems, defoliating and decorticating them (Figure 15e), and soaking the bark strips in water until the water becomes mucilaginous (approximately 10 to 15 min; Figure 15f). The mucilage is strained through mosquito netting or cloth to remove any impurities and then mixed into the fiber-water suspension. The same vạt pạ tissue can be re-soaked in water again up to 10 times to yield formation aid (Dương Văn Quảng, personal communication, October 26, 2022).

5.3.3 Sheet Formation and Drying

Sheet formation for haupau, as for dó liệt, involves pouring buckets of fiber onto a wooden frame of stretched mesh (Figure 15g). However, unlike dó liệt moulds, haupau moulds are wooden, usually made from *dẻ* (*Castanopsis boisii* Hickel & A.Camus) trees, and the porous center consists of stretched cheesecloth rather than mosquito netting. The cheesecloth can last up to 2 years stretched on the moulds before needing replacement. Haupau moulds are made in different sizes, with the largest ones measuring 100 cm by 150 cm (James Ojascastro, personal communication, November 11, 2022). Sheet formation occurs with the mould manipulated close to the ground: small moulds can be manipulated by one person, but the largest moulds require two people, squatting on opposite sides, to operate: one papermaker pours the fiber suspension onto the cheesecloth, and then the papermaker and an assistant immediately grasp opposite ends of the longer poles of the frame, tilting it to distribute the fibers evenly over the netting until all the water and excess formation aid have drained through the mesh. The frame with the wet haupau fiber on it is put in the sun to dry (Figure 15h). In a day, Mr Quảng can make up to 50 sheets of paper: he makes all sheets over the course of the morning, and then leaves them to dry in the sun during the afternoon. However, he normally only makes a few hundred sheets per year, and never more than 1,000 sheets annually (Dương Văn Quảng, personal communication, October 26, 2022). The cost per sheet varies by size: as of 2022, Mr. Quảng charges 50,000 VND (about $2 USD) for smaller sheets (45 cm × 90 cm), while the largest sheets (100 cm × 150 cm) are worth three times as much.

5.4 Uses

Haupau papermaking appears to be a uniquely Cao Lan tradition, made in Khe Nghè to serve local cultural and artistic needs. However, since both the Cao Lan and Nùng are closely-related Tai-speaking ethnic groups sharing similar religious and cultural traditions, it is not surprising to see very similar uses for both Cao Bằng dưỡng and haupau papers.

5.4.1 Burning

As with many ethnic groups across Việt Nam, one such need was ritual burning. Like the Dao Tiền and Nùng, the Cao Lan once carved wooden stamps for embossing handmade votive papers. But instead of shapes and patterns, Cao Lan stamps are carved with the likenesses of an animal emblematic of a Cao Lan family or clan (Figure 15i). The family animal talisman was then embossed onto sheets of haupau, and the stamped papers burned. However, as with Mường uses for their dưởng paper, cheaper, machine-made, and printed wood-pulp sheets have displaced haupau for use as votive paper, and Cao Lan families no longer practice stamp carving and paper embossing.

5.4.2 Writing

Today, haupau paper is chiefly used for recording Cao Lan family history books (Figure 15j). The entire book is made of haupau; thinner sheets are cut and folded to form the pages, while thicker sheets are cut into strips, twisted into paper thread, and used to form the binding. Elders then use brush and ink to record family genealogy in the Cao Lan language, which uses Chinese characters. In addition, since haupau has exemplary ink retention, Cao Lan painters and calligraphers also use this paper for their art. This versatility has made haupau highly sought-after across northern Việt Nam, and customers have come from as far as Quảng Ninh, Hải Phòng, and Hà Nội purchase it (Hồng, 2019). However, due to competition with machine-made papers and increasing scarcity of the haupau liana, continued manufacture of haupau for use outside of Khe Nghè and its Cao Lan inhabitants is uncertain.

5.5 Current Status

According to Dương Văn Quảng, only he and two other artisans still make haupau paper in Khe Nghè Village, though no historical records of the number of papermakers in Cao Lan villages are available. The tiny number of active Cao Lan papermakers today likely reflects the recent and precipitous global decline in hand papermaking due to the widespread replacement of handmade papers with machine-made papers. To ensure Cao Lan handmade paper-based religious and artistic traditions continue for at least one more generation, Mr. Quảng continues to teach his son haupau papermaking. Still, with his son as yet undecided if he will continue making haupau once his father retires, the long-term survival of this unique and highly endemic papermaking tradition remains uncertain.

6. DÓ TRẦM

Aquilaria crassna **Pierre ex Lecomte**
Family Thymelaeaceae

Dó trầm is a rare tree native to the Indochinese Peninsula and Malesia. It is tall but slow growing, attaining a height of 20 m over the course of 80 years (although individuals 49 m tall have been recorded). It bears elliptical leaves with entire margins that are arranged alternately on its branches.

Dó trầm is just one species in the genus *Aquilaria*, a taxon of 15 species (three present in Việt Nam) of tall rainforest trees collectively called agarwood, aloeswood, and gaharu. All *Aquilaria*, along with members of the closely related genus *Gonystylus*, produce a fragrant and highly-sought-after resin used as a defense to fungal infection. Most reports cite the mold *Phaeoacremonium parasiticum* as the principal causative agent inciting *Aquilaria* to produce resin, although several other fungal genera (including *Trichoderma, Fusarium,* and *Cladosporium*) have also been isolated from resinous dó trầm heartwood (Premalatha & Kalra, 2013). Infected trees are harvested for this resinous wood, called agarwood, aloeswood, oud, or oudh, which is sold for high prices to make perfume and incense. Consequently, dó trầm is extremely rare in the wild and is now listed as Critically Endangered by the International Union for the Conservation of Nature (IUCN), and trade of agarwood is controlled by the Convention on International Trade in Endangered Species of Wild Fauna and Flora (CITES, 1994). Nevertheless, illicit harvest of *Aquilaria* is increasing and the threat of its extinction remains high (Soehartono & Newton, 2000, 2001).

Like many of its relatives in the Thymelaeaceae, *Aquilaria* also has sufficiently long (3.7–4.6 mm) cellulosic phloem fibers suitable for papermaking, albeit shorter than dó (6–7 mm) and dướng (6–12 mm) phloem fibers (Barrett, 1983; Ilvessalo-Pfäffli, 1995; Luo et al., 2018; Nguyễn, 2002). These fibers, which also are reportedly not as strong as those from dó (Triệu Văn Thanh, personal communication, January 5, 2019), are whiter and harder and thus provide an excellent writing and painting surface. In both China and Việt Nam, *Aquilaria* fibers were often blended with other fibers before forming sheets: in China, the additive fibers were derived from bamboo to make coarse, buff-colored sheets (McClure, 1986), while in

Việt Nam, they were mixed with dó to produce strong, high-quality ivory-colored papers without the use of bleach.

Although details regarding resinwood harvest are comparatively well-documented, mentions of dó trầm bark harvest for artisan papermaking in the literature remain largely speculative. Presumably this is because the logging of dó trầm trees for fragrance and incense is so lucrative that papermakers have had neither the requisite raw material nor a competitive profit margin to make dó trầm paper. Only a few sources—mostly anecdotal (Helman-Ważny, 2014; Laroque, 2020; Li, 2018)—report the use of dó trầm and other *Aquilaria* species (e.g., *A. sinensis* [Lour.] Spreng.) for making paper. These scarce claims span a wide geographic range, from the foothills of northeastern India to southern China and northern Indochina, with sheets being formed using either float moulds or bamboo screens depending on the region. Almost nothing is definitively known about harvesting techniques, but we surmise that various methods, including bark harvest and branch harvest, were probably used at different times and places throughout the natural range of the *Aquilaria* genus. Given the sparse but recurring attestations regarding the usage of *Aquilaria* for papermaking, one would expect at least a few surviving *Aquilaria* artifacts, but despite an extensive literature search, we were able to identify only two credible examples—a 15th-century manuscript discovered in what is now Nepal (Trier, 1972), and a coarse sheet mixed with bamboo fiber in Floyd McClure's collection used for ritual burning, for lining coffins, and as an insect- and water-repellent wrapping for unripe bitter melons growing on the vine (McClure, 1986). Indeed, not even Kew Gardens reports *Aquilaria* among their 300+ paper artifacts within its extensive ethnobotany collection (Prendergast, 2002). Despite this paucity of physical evidence, oral testimonies reflecting traditional ecological knowledge provide compelling evidence to the historical importance of dó trầm in papermaking, and they ultimately even help to inform ongoing efforts to revive dó trầm usage for artisan paper today.

According to the Dao Tiền dó bark harvesters of Đà Bắc, who harvest dó through complete decortication of entire trunks, the best way to obtain papermaking fiber from dó trầm trees is instead through partial bark harvest. Rather than girdling the entire trunk, harvesters should make short horizontal cuts approximately at breast height, and then rip long strips of bark off one side of the trunk while leaving bark on the other side intact (Triệu Văn Thanh, personal communication, January 5, 2019; Triệu Phúc Thìn, personal communication, November 2, 2022; Figure 16). Since dó trầm trees can regenerate bark more readily than they can regenerate an entire trunk, this method of harvest has the advantage of ensuring a regular supply of fiber without killing an entire, slow-growing tree (Triệu Văn Thanh, personal communication, January 5, 2019; Triệu Phúc Thìn, personal communication, November 2, 2022). These harvesting nuances are especially critical given the concerning decline of dó trầm populations, which is overwhelmingly driven by an insatiable demand for oud. Indeed, in Đà Bắc, dó trầm was once more common than dó (Triệu Văn Thanh, personal communication, January 5, 2019), but the populations there have since dwindled to just 40 trees today

Figure 16. Harvesting methods of dó trầm (*Aquilaria crassna*). a) Triệu Phúc Thìn demonstrating how dó trầm bark is harvested: first, a horizontal incision is made in the bark near breast height, and b) then bark above the incision is torn away from the tree until the strip falls from the canopy. c) A harvested tree, showing the exposed white wood underneath. d) Outer bark. e) Inner bark, showing the very white fibers. Photos d, e by Trần Hồng Nhung.

(Trần Hồng Nhung, personal communication, July 4, 2022). As a result, the Dao Tiền bark harvesters have not made dó trầm paper in over 4 decades, and only now is a very careful and cautious revival being considered.

Starting in 2020, Zó Project began providing logistical and financial support to Dao Tiền bark harvesters in Đà Bắc so they can re-learn their historic tradition of papermaking with dó and dó trầm fiber. This was a challenging and risky but opportune investment because, due to the COVID-19 pandemic, artisan papermaking in Việt Nam ground to a standstill; the papermakers in Bắc Ninh were unable to sell any paper and, as a result, they did not buy any dó fiber from Dao Tiền bark harvesters either. With little money and lots of persistence, some Dao Tiền bark harvesters, like Triệu Phúc Thìn, started learning seo technique from the Mường dướng papermakers in Suối Cỏ. By 2022, these newly trained Dao Tiền artisans began producing their first dó and dó trầm sheets in more than 4 decades. While promising, maintaining this revival will require additional research to quantify key metrics, including harvesting intensity and harvesting frequency, to ensure that dó trầm papermaking is locally sustainable in the long term. Moreover, given the CITES listing of the *Aquilaria* genus, trade and export of dó trầm paper would be subject to stringent regulation, likely constraining this particular revival to use and application within Việt Nam (CITES, 1994).

Despite the logistical and scientific challenges in ensuring sustainability of any use of a critically endangered and tightly regulated species such as dó trầm, there are nevertheless opportunities available for future development of dó trầm papermaking. With *Aquilaria* being so heavily exploited in the wild for resin, entrepreneurs have now turned to growing dó trầm in cultivation and then infecting them artificially with fungus to induce the creation of resinous wood (Azren et al., 2019; Liu et al., 2013). Although this is both costly and time consuming, it is becoming an increasingly common method of producing agarwood due to the rarity of the wild tree and the steep prices consumers are willing to pay for fragrances. Given the fact that fragrance industries only use the wood and hand papermakers only use the inner bark, a sustainable local byproduct economy of hand papermaking traditions using dó trầm bark fibers may be possible. However, further networking between dó trầm growers in the fragrance industry and hand papermakers in northern Việt Nam is needed, and with assurance that it is done legally and in compliance with domestic and international regulations.

7. CONSERVATION

Despite a history of papermaking spanning at least 17 centuries, Việt Nam today is at grave risk of losing its unique and diverse paper arts heritage. As with Japan (Barrett, 1983) and Korea (Lee, 2012), the greatest threat to hand papermaking in Việt Nam is displacement by machine-made, wood-pulp paper industries, which produce cheaper (but often lower-quality) papers at large scales. Fortunately, for some artistic, cultural, and conservation-related purposes, machine-made paper cannot replace handmade paper, ensuring that a small but persistent demand for handmade paper continues even today. As a result, just a few bark harvesters, papermakers, and paper artists left in Việt Nam continue participating in this tiny artisanal economy today. Together they form a fragile production chain, where loss of any single link in the transformation of a plant into a handmade paper product risks the total collapse of Vietnamese paper arts traditions: Đông Hồ paintings cannot be made without dó paper, dó paper cannot be made if dó bark is not harvested, and, as is the case with dó specifically over the past century, without harvesters, papermakers, and artists, the paper plants themselves become less common, with no one interested or capable left to cultivate or manage them.

Despite its precipitous decline and precarious present status, Vietnamese papermaking and paper arts can still survive and even thrive through the 21st century, but urgent and coordinated support is necessary. Fortunately, neither bark harvest, nor hand papermaking, nor most kinds of Vietnamese paper arts, have gone extinct completely, and even in places where they are no longer practiced, there are usually still elders alive who retain critical traditional ecological and artisanal knowledge that can be shared and leveraged to revive recently lost practices. However, since Vietnamese paper arts are the product of a complex, stepwise, and interconnected process (Figure 17) involving the application of such specialized knowledge by just a few highly trained people, it is essential that conservation efforts are broadly supportive of the whole system and not just a single step or agent therein. Creative support systems—both domestic and international—are therefore needed to conserve Vietnamese paper arts, but it is also imperative that these support systems complement, rather than displace, these unique and threatened traditions. To insure against network failure, we therefore recommend three strategies to maintain connectivity and functionality in the Vietnamese traditional paper arts economy: 1) to reinforce existing but weakening connections; 2) to restore extinct connections; and 3) to create new connections. We present examples of each strategy below, and we recommend applying all three simultaneously for the effective long-term conservation of Vietnamese hand papermaking and paper arts traditions.

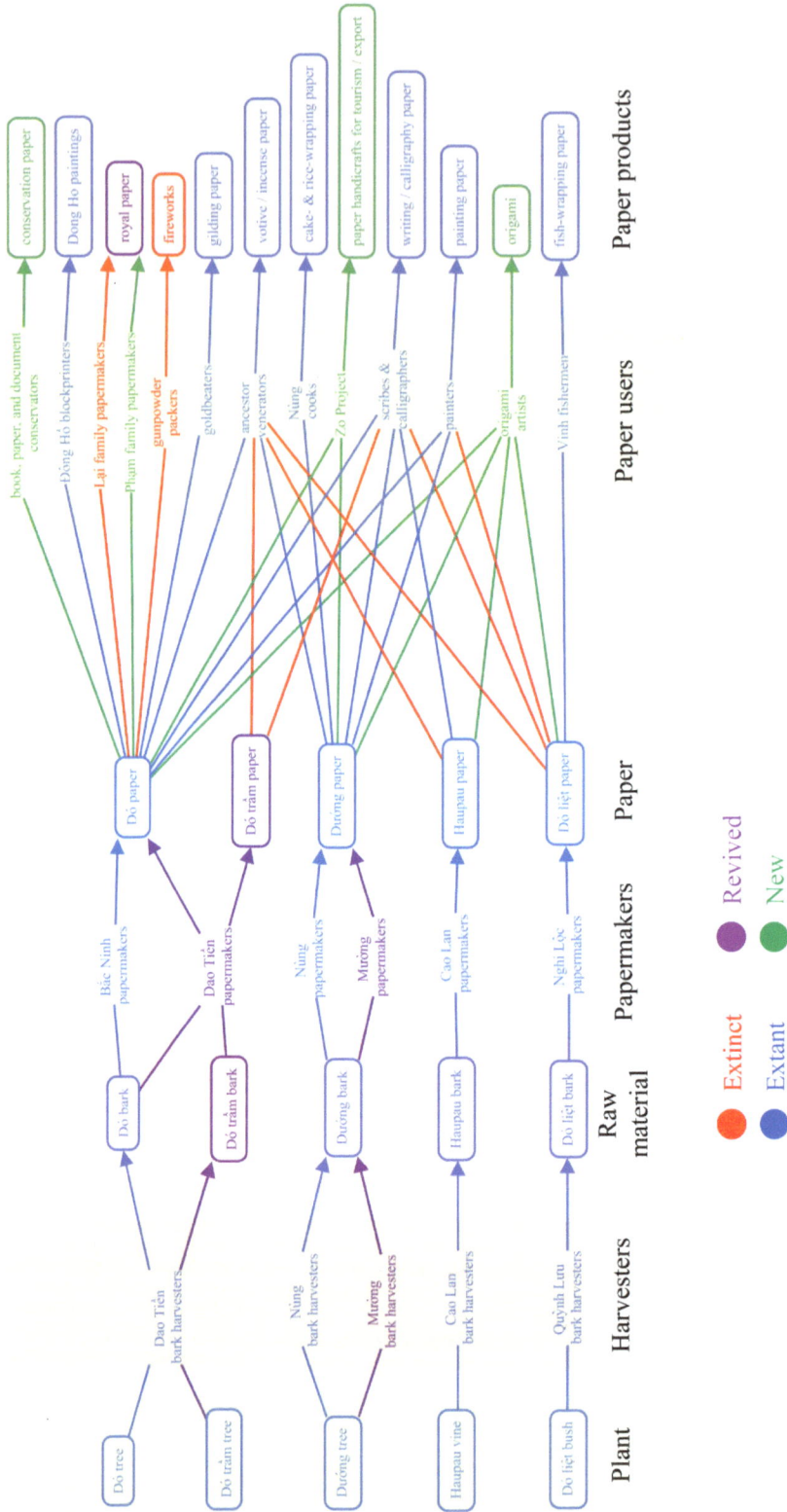

Figure 17. Economy of artisanal papermaking and papercrafts in Việt Nam. Red text, arrows, and polygons denote components and processes that no longer participate in the artisanal paper economy; blue denotes those that are still extant; purple denotes those that went extinct but were revived and reintegrated; and green denotes those that are recent additions and integrations. Bark harvesters and papermakers are described by location if they are Kinh, and by ethnic group otherwise.

7.1 Reinforcing Extant Connections

Whether for a threatened species, threatened language, or threatened ethnobotanical tradition, the first step to effective conservation is documentation. Accessible documentation provides insurance against further knowledge loss by providing fixed media (text or audio-visual) to complement existing (oral and manual) pathways of transmitting knowledge. As we showed in the introduction, Việt Nam has no comprehensive manual, handbook, or monograph on papermaking traditions, and those recorded here and in subsequent planned publications in both English and Vietnamese can be a reference for learning and teaching in perpetuity.

One avenue we expanded to improve the documentation of Vietnamese paper arts is through the purchase and preservation of physical objects. Through our fieldwork in Việt Nam, the first (J.O.) and third (T.H.N.) authors purchased numerous papers and papermaking paraphernalia during collaborative fieldwork for use, preservation, and study in perpetuity at the Zó Project studio in EcoPark, Hà Nội and the William L. Brown Center at the Missouri Botanical Garden in St. Louis, Missouri—facilities which collectively continue to provide active and accessible conservation of papermaking and ethnobotanical knowledge both within Việt Nam and ex situ in the United States. Detailed metadata on the Vietnamese paper and papermaking artifacts maintained at the Brown Center are available online through the Tropicos database (www.tropicos.org), and at the end of this monograph in Appendix B.

Documentation, however, is not by itself sufficient for conservation; money and support systems are also needed to ensure economic solvency of artisanal traditions. Documentation cannot be relied upon to convey all the knowledge a papermaker uses when sheet-forming. The motions of an expert papermaker—which also vary subtly from papermaker to papermaker—involve unspoken nuance, drawn from decades of practice and cannot be condensed both comprehensively and digestibly in a written primer (Barrett, 1983). Even with the right tools and copious written documentation, students inevitably fall short in learning artisanal traditions and cannot replicate the work of the master without extensive apprenticeship. This is because craft manuals and monographs usually only describe what should be done to produce an artisanal product, but mastering a craft requires learning what *should not* be done too (Koretsky & Koretsky, 1991; Lee, 2012). As outsiders, we only see the "successes" of an artisan through their finished products, but achieving this caliber of skill requires years of learning from failure and mistakes—a journey unseen to all except the artisans themselves.

Practitioners and documentation offer complementary repositories of knowledge: just as a music student best learns Vivaldi with both sheet music and a music teacher, papermaking students must still be able to apprentice from master papermakers and not solely from monographs such as this one. Consequently, workshops and apprenticeship programs are urgently needed to ensure direct transmission and prevent further declines in Vietnamese traditional papermaking. Fortunately, successful case studies for organizing, funding, and regulating artisan papermaking industries exist, and these examples can serve as models for effective conservation of threatened paper arts traditions in Việt Nam.

Like any other enterprise, hand papermaking industries benefit from economic investment, which may come from the government or the private sector. In most cases, governmental contributions to traditional papermaking have been symbolic rather than financial, but when the government does provide grants or subsidies to support papermakers, it can fund development of infrastructure to allow organization and regulation of artisanal traditions like papermaking. More abstractly, government support of papermaking helps to cultivate and reinforce national (and even international) recognition and pride that paper arts are a part of a country's artistic heritage. For example, in Nepal, papermaking as an artisanal profession was declining during the middle of the 20th century. The royal family, which saw lokta paper as emblematic of Nepal and historically used lokta for royal decrees and edicts, commissioned field studies to explore best harvesting and management practices of lokta plants for use in artisanal papermaking at a national scale (Jeanrenaud, 1983). Following these feasibility studies, the growing number of papermakers then banded together to form Nepal Handmade Paper Association (HANDPASS), a guild that regulates artisanal papermaking throughout Nepal and promotes it overseas. Although the guild is separate from the government (and receives no direct funding from it), membership in HANDPASS requires government registration. Today, several hundred hand papermaking industries are registered with the Government of Nepal (Biggs & Messerschmidt, 2005), and Nepalese handmade paper remains a very popular export to art suppliers around the world. Similar papermakers' associations also exist in Japan—including the Sekishu-Banshi Craftsmen's Association, the Association for the Preservation of Hon-minoshi Papermaking, and the Hosokawa-shi Craftsmen's Association—to promote the continued manufacture of washi (Japanese handmade paper); these, however, tend to operate at more regional and local than national scales (United Nations Educational, Scientific and Cultural Organization [UNESCO], 2014). And governmental recognition may even be bestowed at the individual level, but only to the most highly skilled and experienced artisans whose knowledge may be irreplaceable: for example, the designation of papermaker Sajio Hamada as a living national treasure of Japan (Seki, 2013).

Government support can also draw income from the private sector, chiefly through tourism. In Mexico, for example, the Ministry of Tourism began designating towns with significant natural beauty or historical significance as "*pueblos mágicos*" to draw tourists (and their spending money) into more rural parts of the country. One pueblo mágico in the state of Puebla, Pahuatlán, is right across the San Marcos River from San Pablito, the sole remaining village in the world that still makes amate (Mexico's indigenous paper, which is made by hand without aqueous dispersion of constituent fibers in a vat). While San Pablito itself is not a pueblo mágico, its proximity to Pahuatlán ensures that a steady stream of tourists patronize the amateros (people who make amate) throughout the year to participate in amate workshops and to buy decorative amate crosses, bookmarks, cards, lampshades, and tapestries (León & Ojascastro, 2024). Even minimal government involvement—in this case, a symbolic designation—can draw real money to artisans living in remote places and help ensure they pass on their craft knowledge to the next generation of artisans.

Finally, artisanal support can even be intergovernmental. UNESCO, a branch of the United Nations, has compiled two Lists of Intangible Cultural Heritage, both intended to safeguard key examples of cultural diversity and creative expression around the world (UNESCO, 2003). The larger of these two lists, the Representative List of the Intangible Cultural Heritage of Humanity, showcases the diversity of human expression through food, song, dance, celebration, religion, ritual, and craftsmanship. A second list, the List of Intangible Cultural Heritage in Need of Urgent Safeguarding, compiles notable traditions that are under grave threat of extinction. Five hundred eighty-four traditions combined are represented in both lists, and of these, only two directly concern papermaking: the manufacture of washi in Japan, and xuan papermaking in China. And although UNESCO lists 14 Vietnamese traditions (one in Need of Urgent Safeguarding), none concern paper arts, despite Việt Nam's extensive papermaking history. Unfortunately, while these UNESCO designations are coveted, they do not confer any money to assist in the preservation or conservation of these unique cultural traditions and heritages. Further international advocacy is therefore needed to bring greater attention—and especially money—to ensure these diverse, unique, and vulnerable papermaking traditions continue to be practiced across northern Việt Nam.

So far, small, intermittent government support has been provided for Vietnamese papermakers. This has included small, one-time grants to the Cao Lan artisans who make haupau paper in Bắc Giang, and to the woodcarvers and printers who make Đông Hồ paintings in Bắc Ninh. However, this by itself is not enough to support artisans full-time.

Since Vietnamese state-owned newspapers and magazines regularly publish articles on Vietnamese crafts in both Vietnamese and English, profiled artisans often receive subsequent attention by tourists, tour groups, and visiting artists. While this kind of trickle-down strategy has been in use in Mexico, Japan, and Nepal for several decades, it is still underdeveloped in Việt Nam, which opened to tourists relatively late (in 1987), delayed by war and subsequent economic reforms. Currently, artisans living and operating close to Hà Nội tend to have better economic mobility because they have easier access to selling their handmade paper and paper products to international tourists in the capital, while those that live in very remote places and make paper for local use see essentially no economic benefit in sales of paper and papercrafts to visitors. And although continued globalization may improve the ability of rural papermakers to sell products to a much wider market, it also tends to draw younger generations away from artisanal disciplines with increasing accessibility to higher paying, alternative trades and careers. Furthermore, it should be mentioned that tourism cannot be the sole measure to ensure that hand papermaking traditions remain solvent, because some artisans will not welcome the attention and infrastructural and economic changes associated with tourism. Financial investment from a variety of sources and applied mindfully with engagement from (and addressing the needs of) each artisan community is therefore essential to ensuring that Vietnamese paper arts traditions continue to be practiced through the 21ˢᵗ century.

One organization that's very active in empowering Vietnamese papermakers and bark harvesters is Zó Project, a social enterprise founded in 2013 by the second author (T.H.N.). Over the past decade, Ms. Nhung has authored numerous articles describing Vietnamese paper arts, collaborated with Vietnamese paper artists in shows and exhibitions in Hà Nội, and connected Vietnamese papermakers with international customers to help them earn much-needed supplemental income. Her efforts continue to help extant Vietnamese papermaking and paper arts traditions survive in an increasingly globalized and digitized world.

7.2 Restoring Extinct Connections

The most rapid erosion of papermaking knowledge in Việt Nam occurred during the 2 decades since the end of the war with the United States. During this postwar period, Việt Nam transitioned into a globalized market economy under the doctrine of Đổi Mới, and large factories using heavy, automated machinery began rapidly displacing the manual craft and artisan economies village by village (Fanchette, 2016; Fanchette & Stedman, 2009; Peachey, 1995). Unable to compete with cheaper, machine-made wood-pulp paper, thousands of hand papermakers abandoned their trade, and only a few dozen artisans still make paper by hand in Việt Nam today. Although many parts of the Vietnamese hand papermaking economy still have some tiny number of participants today, several critical aspects have become extinct entirely. Unlike with species extinctions, tradition extinctions are a slower death, eroding in stages usually first with the cessation of the practice, followed many years later by the death of the last practitioner (Pang, 1992; Schattenburg-Raymond, 2020). Feasibility of papermaking revival therefore depends on two principal factors, in order of increasing importance: first, the survival of paper artifacts, tools, and/or accompanying historical records or documentation and second, the survival of people having experiential knowledge of papermaking and paper arts methods that are no longer practiced. Both factors continue to be leveraged to help restore connectivity in the fragile Vietnamese artisan papermaking economy.

The feasibility of reviving lost traditions is proportional to the quality and quantity of evidence of how the tradition existed. Once again, there are case studies that serve as precedents and may inform strategies to revive extinct or locally extirpated practices in Vietnamese paper arts. Perhaps the best model we have of a fiber-based artisan tradition being resurrected is the case of kapa in Hawai'i, a type of barkcloth made primarily from felted paper mulberry fibers that went extinct around 1900 and was subsequently revived—some 7 decades later (Schattenburg-Raymond, 2020).

Given the sheer length of time when no kapa was made in Hawai'i, no old kapa-maker was alive to tutor a new generation of artisans when interest in the tradition began brewing again during the 1970s. Reviving kapa manufacture therefore had to proceed through diligent scholarship of extant historical and artefactual records from the early 20th century and before. Fortunately, hundreds of precolonial kapa artifacts—alongside many kapa-making tools, mostly fiber beaters—still survive in Hawai'i, in large part due to the conservation and curatorial work of the Bishop Museum (Pang, 1992). Extensive (though sometimes conflicting) accounts of kapa-making survive too—from European and Hawai'ian ethnographers and historians. And finally, kapa in Hawai'i is related to broader Austronesian traditions of making barkcloth, so loss of knowledge in Hawai'i could be supplemented by studying barkcloth-making traditions still practiced across neighboring Polynesian islands. Together, these considerations provided a sufficiently critical mass of knowledge to allow for the successful revival of kapa-making traditions in Hawai'i, which are still practiced and taught to this day (Bell, 1985; Schattenburg-Raymond, 2020). This case study is not unique to barkcloth; successful revival of the related paper-like daluang tradition in Indonesia—which, like kapa, is made from paper mulberry—also proceeded similarly, with artifacts, written histories, and neighboring extant papermaking and barkcloth-making methods contributing to the reification of Indonesian beaten-bark paper today (Miles, 2019).

Remarkably, despite decades of war followed by rapid economic change, many communities in Việt Nam still retain critical papermaking and paper arts knowledge. However, since surviving Vietnamese papermaking knowledge is fragmentary and spread across diverse communities, extinct knowledge endemic to a particular ethnic group might need to be borrowed and adapted from another. The revival of dướng papermaking among the Mường ethnic group is especially notable in this regard because, unlike the Dao Tiến villages in Đà Bắc, there were no living papermakers belonging to their ethnic group available as a resource to train or inform aspiring paper artisans on how to make paper. Furthermore, no historic Mường papermaking tools survived in usable condition for contemporary papermaking. Consequently, Mường artisans had to co-opt related knowledge from other papermaking traditions, and then tailor them to their own needs. By combining Japanese sheet formation methods (designed for washi), Kinh papermaking tools (designed for dó), oral accounts of Mường paper arts, and adequate time and financial support, Mường artisans were able to recreate dướng paper very similar to those their ancestors made generations before. This success with Mường papermaking sets a useful and inspirational precedent for reviving other paper arts traditions elsewhere in Việt Nam.

By comparison, communities that still retain living keepers of traditional ecological knowledge are generally better positioned for reviving recently extinct cultural traditions. For example, Đà Bắc, which stopped making paper around 1980, still has former papermakers living there; of these, at least one has the (still functional) liềm seo he used 4 decades earlier (Triệu Văn Thanh, personal communication, January 5, 2019). Despite no longer being practiced, both material and methodological papermaking knowledge is still extant in Đà Bắc. Furthermore, Dao Tiền youths are enthusiastic about the prospect of relearning their papermaking heritage using both dó and dó trầm as raw materials. So, starting in 2020, the second author (T.H.N.) and her social enterprise Zó Project brought the Mường papermakers from Suối Cỏ, and liềm seo and khung seo from Bắc Ninh, to Đà Bắc to help the Dao Tiền communities revive their papermaking and paper arts traditions. And like the Mường before them, the Dao Tiền applied and tailored introduced tools and methods to their own flora and prior artisanal knowledge to materialize their otherwise lost traditions, resulting in unique convergences. For example, in lieu of using mò or a synthetic formation aid, Dao Tiền papermakers add a mucilage extracted from a vine which they call **mò dây**; this vine, it turns out, is the same species (*Byttneria aspera*) as the khổ háo vine used for formation aid by the Nùng papermakers 400 km away. Within just 2 years, and during the COVID-19 pandemic no less, Dao Tiền artisans had already begun making their own paper for local use and for export. But more research and development are still needed to continue refining and scaling this newly revived Dao Tiền tradition, especially regarding how dó trầm harvesting frequency, harvesting intensity, and paper applications compare to those of dó. Furthermore, other promising fiber plants, like the vining dướng congener *Broussonetia kaempferi* (Figure 18a) and the woody hemp relative **hu đay** (*Trema orientale* [L.] Blume; Figure 18b), grow in Đà Bắc too, but their suitability for paper there is still yet to be explored. The bark of a third tree, **duối** (*Streblus asper* Lour.; Figure 18c), which does not grow in Đà Bắc but grows elsewhere in northern Việt Nam (e.g., Suối Cỏ), has historical precedent in hand papermaking in both Siam and Cambodia (Beckett, 1888; Boonpitaksakul et al., 2019; Hunter, 1936) to make folded, accordion-style books (Thai: **samut**; Khmer: **kraing**), some of which still survive today. Interestingly, some French officials claim duối bark was also used to make paper in Tonkin, but no duối paper artifacts from Việt Nam are known to exist today (Crevost & Lémarié, 1920; Laroque, 2020). Regardless of whether duối was used in Vietnamese paper-

Figure 18. Novel plants to consider for bark-based hand papermaking in Việt Nam today. a) Dó dây (*Broussonetia kaempferi*), Đà Bắc. Hòa Bình Province. b) Hu đay (*Trema orientale*), Đà Bắc. Hòa Bình Province. c) Duối (*Streblus asper*), Suối Cỏ, Hòa Bình Province. Photo c by Trần Hồng Nhung.

making historically, it still grows throughout Việt Nam today and can be harvested where available for artisanal papermaking and paper art.

7.3 Creating New Connections

Historically, hand papermaking traditions persisted by provisioning paper mostly for local use. Although a few traditions, like Nùng dướng and Cao Lan haupau, still operate this way, cheap, machine-made wood-pulp paper has wholly displaced handmade paper for daily use nearly everywhere today. Fortunately, the collective resilience of hand papermaking traditions is derived from their non-substitutability. Đông Hồ paintings can only be printed on dó, and Cao Lan ancestor books can only be written on and bound with haupau. This non-substitutability can be leveraged beyond local economies and adopted to other purposes that similarly require high-quality, handmade papers. By connecting hand papermaking traditions to niche but novel specialty applications, traditional papermakers and paper artists in their respective crafts can be more strongly incentivized to continue and pass on their papermaking knowledge—first by expanding the pool of potential customers from local to global, and second by capitalizing on the premium many customers in the Global North are willing to pay for handmade or artisanal products. This can drive not only the co-optation of Vietnamese paper for preexisting arts (origami), but also the synthesis of new—and entirely Vietnamese—art (Trúc Chỉ).

7.3.1 Origami

In one example of a potentially new art form, as mentioned earlier, artist Nguyễn Hùng Cường pioneered the adaptation of dó paper for origami (Figure 19a), but this innovation is not limited to dó fibers, nor is it constrained to art in Việt Nam. Thanks to distribution efforts by Zó Project (Việt Nam) and Origamishop (France), all Vietnamese handmade papers except dó trầm are now available internationally, and origami artists around the world can now directly compare different Vietnamese fibers for folding. For example, Mr. Cường finds the smoothness, shininess, and refinement of his favorite paper—dó—exceptionally well-suited to his style of origami; these properties, plus crispness, are further enhanced through sizing with PVA glue and acrylic paint. American origamist Beth Moore Johnson agrees, and she has found similar success sizing and pigmenting her dó-based designs using acrylic paint mixed with methylcellulose instead of PVA (Beth Moore Johnson, personal communication, January 8, 2023; Figure 19b). However, fellow American origamist Jared Needle does not prefer dó, as he finds that it is susceptible to tearing when used with watery sizing agents like methylcellulose (Jared Needle, personal communication, January 7, 2023; Figure 19c).

Our understanding of the properties and personalities of the lesser-known Vietnamese handmade papers are also enhanced through the medium of origami. Mr. Cường praises

Figure 19. Contemporary artworks using Vietnamese handmade papers. a) "Great White Shark," designed, folded, and photographed by Nguyễn Hùng Cường, from one uncut square of dó paper, 2013. b) "Owls," designed, folded, and photographed by Beth Moore Johnson, from uncut squares of dó paper painted with acrylics before folding, 2019. c) "Maris the Otter," designed, folded, and photographed by Jared Needle, from one uncut square of dó paper, 2018. d) "Rat," designed, folded, and photographed by Nguyễn Hùng Cường, from dướng paper dyed with logwood before folding, 2020. e) "Mice Stealing Egg," designed, folded, and photographed by Nguyễn Anh Nghĩa, from dướng paper dyed with logwood before folding, 2020. f) "Tarantula," designed, folded, and photographed by Cekouat Elím León Peralta, from one uncut square of dó liệt paper treated with methylcellulose, 2020. g) "Cyriopalus 3.5," designed, folded, and photographed by Nguyễn Hùng Cường, from one uncut square of dó liệt paper, 2022. h) "Bactrian Camel," designed by Shuki Kato, folded and photographed by Ryan Charpentier, from one uncut square of haupau paper, 2020. i) "Love Symbol #2," designed, folded, and photographed by James Ojascastro, from one uncut square of duo haupau (white) + lokta (purple) paper, 2021.

(Mường) dướng paper for its strength and whiteness (obtained through bleaching), though he dislikes the stiffness and roughness of the constituent fibers (Figure 19d). Another Vietnamese origamist, Nguyễn Anh Nghĩa, likes the heterogeneity in thickness and texture of dướng paper, which he says adds organic and animated qualities to living subjects (Figure 19e), but he also recognizes that mastering folding with uneven and variable papers can be challenging, especially for novice paperfolders (Nguyễn Anh Nghĩa, personal communication, January 8, 2023). Origamists like Cekouat León Elim Peralta of Mexico (as well as Mr. Cường) recommend dó liệt for origami arthropods (Figure 19f, g), due to its thinness, strength, softness, good performance with methylcellulose for shaping, and availability in large (65 cm × 65 cm) sizes; however, they dislike its relatively unrefined manufacture that involves using old and patched screens, which result in sheets that are bumpy or uneven, and which can detract from the aesthetic appeal of the final model (Cekouat Elim León Peralta, personal communication, January 7, 2023; Nguyễn Hùng Cường, personal communication, January 7, 2023). And for haupau, origamists like Ryan Charpentier (USA) and the first author (J.O.) adore its crispness, thinness, and ease of folding, even without treatment with methylcellulose or polyvinylacetate glue, but are disappointed at its relatively high cost (Ryan Charpentier, personal communication, December 20, 2019; Figure 19h, i). Altogether, although demand for Vietnamese handmade papers for folding origami is still modest (but growing), these recent co-optations have been well received by local papermakers, many of whom have reported to us that they are pleased to learn that the paper they make and sell may eventually turn into beautiful works of art, in both Việt Nam and abroad.

And although co-optation of Vietnamese handmade papers to new purposes has already been successfully and popularly applied to origami, their strength, texture, absorbency, longevity, and acid-free qualities may prove ideal for other artistic and conservation applications still unexplored or underexplored, including cyanotype, letterpress, typewriting, watercolor, bookbinding, and document restoration. By introducing and tailoring Vietnamese paper to new purposes, Vietnamese paper artisans can gain new customers and, therefore, become financially incentivized to remain in their craft industry. This incentive becomes especially lucrative if new customers are affluent or from the Global North—demographics that are more likely both able and willing to pay premiums for handmade, artisanal goods. There is even precedent for such evolution in the traditional paper arts economy; places like Nepal maintain successful hand papermaking industries in large part because as much as 90% of their artisan papers are exported elsewhere for use in scrapbooking, printmaking, letterpress, greeting cards, notebooks, and origami (Subedi et al., 2006), with the remainder still being retained domestically for local uses and traditions. For example, Nepalese government documents and birth certificates are still printed on lokta following a centuries-old tradition (Biggs & Messerschmidt, 2005; Jnawali, 2019). And in Japan, although some handmade paper is still used domestically for construction (as in shoji screens), calligraphy, and painting, many sheets are now exported to Europe and the USA for use in document conservation, because the long kōzō fibers in specialty sheets like tengujo are acid-free, dimensionally stable, and superior for repairing a wide variety of antique documents and books from around the world (Susie Cobbledick, personal communication, 2022). Together, these Nepalese and Japanese case studies show that globalization can be leveraged in ways that empower, rather than extinguish, artisan economies like traditional papermaking.

7.3.2 Trúc Chỉ and Trucchigraphy

Nestled in the center of Việt Nam is the city of Huế, an old imperial city. Huế is home to centuries-old traditions in craft, culture, and history since it holds the stories of the last 13 dynasties in Việt Nam. In this rich environment, a form of contemporary paper art called *Trúc Chỉ* was started in 2010 by Phan Hải Bằng, an artist and lecturer at Huế University. Mr. Hải Bằng received his formal training in papermaking in studios across northern Thailand. These studies were supported in part by a 7-month fieldwork award from the Asian Scholarship Foundation (ASP). At Idin Paper Mill in Chiang Mai, Mr. Hải Bằng studied with master papermaker Supan Promsen (Figure 20a), who taught him traditional saa (*Broussonetia papyrifera*) papermaking as well as contemporary methods like the water blowout technique, which uses water pressure to finely move pulp around a stencil surface (Figure 20b). Mr. Hải Bằng continued working and teaching this form of contemporary papermaking in his studio practice in Huế, incorporating various methods of drawing, printmaking, painting, sculpture, and fiber into his work (Figure 20c). He started teaching this style of contemporary paper art to his students at the University of Huế and at the 1st and 2nd Huế Printmaking Workshop. One of his students, Trần Quang Thắng, fell in love with the process and continued collaborating with Mr. Hải Bằng to develop the craft into a recognized community art project. Later, the professor, writer, and translator, Bửu Ý, formally gave *Trúc Chỉ* its name in 2010. Another colleague of Mr. Hải Bằng's, artist and designer, Ngô Đình Vi, also became involved in the project and is now the manager of Trúc Chỉ Art Project.

Trúc, meaning bamboo in Vietnamese, celebrates the national abundance of this plant and is a symbol of strength for the Vietnamese people. *Chỉ*, meaning paper in Sino-Vietnamese, brings together the term *Trúc Chỉ;* a contemporary paper art form to celebrate paper. Throughout Việt Nam, the ancient uses of paper have always been regarded as a substrate for texts, images, and information, but rarely has the medium been regarded as a form of artwork itself (Phan Hải Bằng, personal communication, 2022), and, compounded by the many political and economic threats to Vietnamese hand papermaking traditions, contemporary paper arts developed within Việt Nam are rare, making Trúc Chỉ an especially valuable innovation (Figure 20d).

Since dó is difficult to source in Huế, the use of local plants is preferred. Paper made at Mr. Hải Bằng's Trúc Chỉ Studio is made from over 50 fibers, including banana, sugarcane, corn, bamboo, coconut, pine needles, lotus stem, lily, pineapple—and to a lesser extent, dó and dướng. Each fiber varies in how it is applied for Trúc Chỉ works. Banana leaves, for ex-

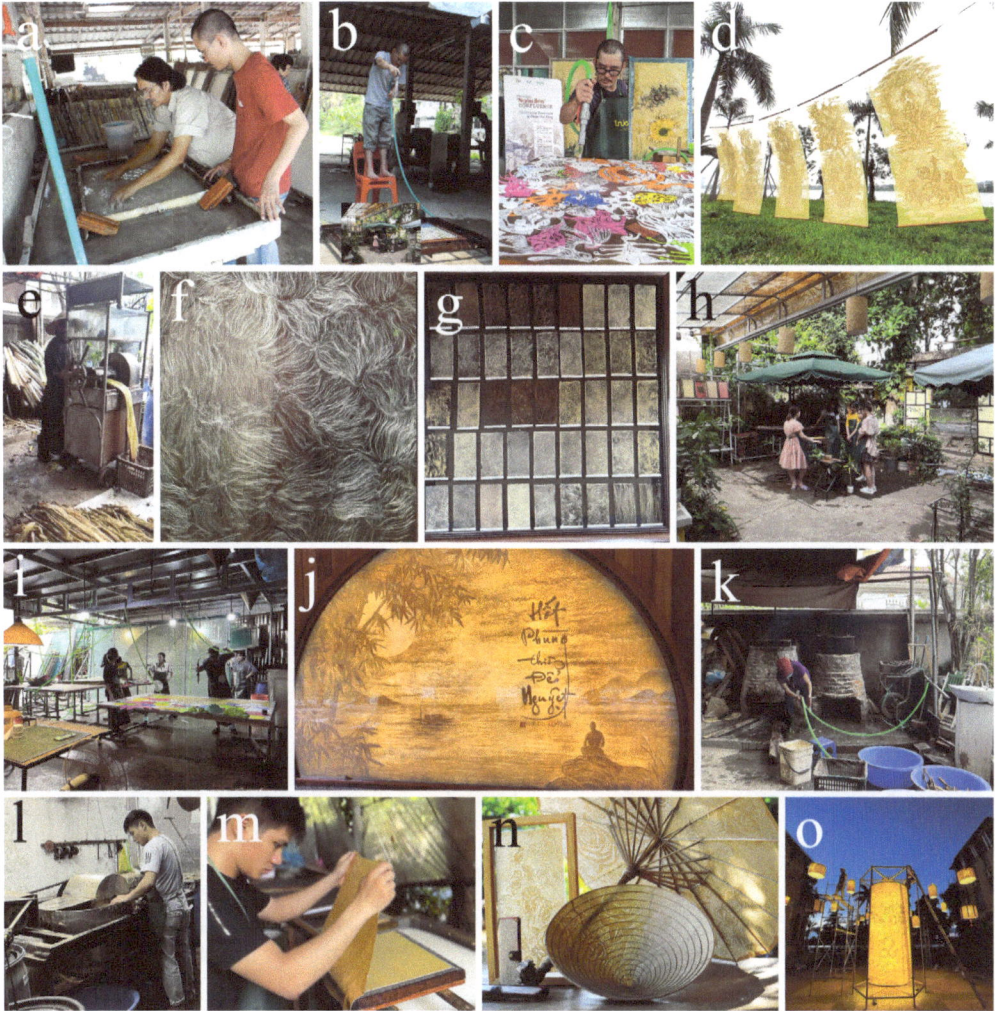

Figure 20. Contemporary Trúc Chỉ artworks and processes. a) Supan Promsen teaching Phan Hải Bằng saa papermaking using the floating mould technique. b) Mr. Hải Bằng using the blowout technique. c) Mr. Hải Bằng working in his studio, October 2022. d) SIPA Biennale, 2012, Phan Hải Bằng. e) Pulping of banana stems using a sugar cane juicing machine, in the papermaking area of the Trúc Chỉ papermaking/print-making lab. f) Detail of banana fibers after processing in a Trúc Chỉ piece. g) Examples of different papers made at the Trúc Chỉ studio. h) Trúc Chỉ gallery during a summer workshop. i) Trúc Chỉ working studio, employees are working on large-scale commission. j) In-process public artwork at the Huyền Không Sơn Thượng Pagoda, Huế, Việt Nam. k) Cooking station at the Trúc Chỉ working studio. l) Hollander beater at the Trúc Chỉ working studio. m) Papermaking technique used at Trúc Chỉ, layering a piece of cotton muslin after pulling a sheet. n) Types of different contemporary Trúc Chỉ product and designs. o) Trúc Chỉ public installation for the Mid-Autumn Moon Festival in Huế, September 2022. Photos a, b, c, d, e, f, n, o by Phan Hải Bằng; photos g, h, i, j, k, l, m by Veronica Y Phạm.

ample, are processed through a sugarcane crusher, and yield long, coarse fibers (Figure 20e). This is used specifically for applications for textural components, adding brushstroke-like marks to each piece (Figure 20f). Shorter fibers, like corn and pineapple, are used to create layers noticeable in many Trúc Chỉ pieces. Shorter fibers are easier to manipulate using the stencil and blowout technique because they are easier to disperse under water pressure. Sometimes fibers are hand beaten to add variety and improve control, resulting in longer fibers and distinctive textures. Dó and dướng are similarly used based on what is needed for certain Trúc Chỉ pieces. Furthermore, there is an emphasis on using locally available plant materials, either intentionally harvested or found discarded, to encourage practitioners to be mindful and deliberate in creating environmentally sustainable artworks (Figure 20g). By leveraging this botanical diversity in an urban setting, Trúc Chỉ allows Vietnamese paper arts to transcend the few plants used for papermaking by tradition in rural parts of Việt Nam, thereby making learning and practicing Vietnamese paper arts accessible to anyone.

Artists and students can participate in studio residencies to learn about Trúc Chỉ, and gain hands-on experience to then incorporate into their own practice. A part of the process involves a technique called **Trucchigraphy**, which combines traditional papermaking techniques, the water-blowout technique, and principles of printmaking to create works of art that reveal layers of imagery on an illuminated surface. Like the idea of calligraphy, the term "Trucchigraphy" was created to emphasize the painterly use of the contemporary art form, Trúc Chỉ. During the summer, there are often summer workshops for students to learn about Trúc Chỉ or artists-in-residence using the facilities (Figure 20h). Here, students can explore the first steps of this craft: learning about the fibers used, forming sheets of paper, and creating stencils for blowout.

The Trúc Chỉ Studio team assembles large-scale public artworks that are being commissioned in Huế and across Việt Nam (Figure 20i). These public works can be seen in pagodas, museums, public parks, and buildings, including the National Assembly House and National Government Office (Figure 20j). The working studio is where most of the processing happens (Figure 20k). Fiber is collected, cooked in traditional lime clay pots, and processed in two different types of beaters (Hollander or naginata), based on what is used for each commission (Figure 20l).

The papermaking and printmaking lab is mostly used for sheet forming, pressing, and drying handmade sheets. Trúc Chỉ papermaking techniques utilize mostly Indian and European sheet forming processes, where a mould and deckle is used. When a sheet is pulled from the vat, the water drains and the deckle is removed, revealing the captured pulp on the mould. Afterward, a thin sheet of cotton muslin is layered over the top before couching the sheet onto the stack (Figure 20m). In the facilities, there is also a printmaking area that holds an etching press to which artists at Trúc Chỉ have access to print their artwork onto paper.

After many years of development, both Phan Hải Bằng and Trúc Chỉ are recognized in Huế and across Việt Nam for their impact on contemporary Vietnamese arts. Mr. Hải Bằng's

Trúc Chỉ Studio continues to be a means of sustainable economic work for the employees there, an educational tool for young artists, and a celebration of paper as a fine art in and of itself (Figure 20n, o).

7.4 Botanical Vouchering

A critical component to documenting and conserving Vietnamese papermaking traditions is a deepened botanical focus. Although our conservation recommendations primarily focus on the papermaking traditions themselves, the traditions cannot exist without the many botanical raw materials we described here. Informed and actionable conservation of key ethnobotanical traditions, like hand papermaking, therefore hinges on informed and accurate identifications of the plants in use. The plants we have described we identified to the best of our ability, and often following consultation with many botanical specialists for Vietnamese flora (including Hoàng Thanh Sơn, Nguyễn Hoàng Nghĩa, and Trịnh Bon) and Thymelaeaceae (Zachary Rogers). In several cases, due to access challenges or the condition of available plants at artisans' studios, determination of plants to species level was simply not possible (e.g., the identification of the "tre" bamboo for making liềm seo). Still, though we feel confident with many of our identifications (even at the species level), they fall short of the accepted best practices for botanical documentation—collecting vouchered plant specimens for storage and curation in herbaria in perpetuity. Herbarium vouchering allows for physical manipulation of plants to identify diagnostic characters for direct comparison with other similar species, and it permits tissue sampling to affirm taxonomic placements through phylogenetic methods. Together, these morphological and genetic evaluations of vouchered specimens permit plant identification with far less ambiguity than solely through pictures. We plan to continue our work in future field seasons to voucher each plant we describe here and revise our descriptions as needed.

8. Conclusion

Our intention with this monograph is twofold: 1) to comprehensively describe Vietnamese bark-based papermaking traditions in a way that is approachable to a wide audience—botanists, anthropologists, and artists alike; and 2) to mobilize the conservation of these severely endangered traditions. As our world continues to be increasingly globalized, mechanized, and digitized, documentation and preservation of artisanal traditions becomes ever more important, especially as practices cease, tools are lost, and elders pass on without transmitting their knowledge. And yet, despite rapid and dramatic changes to societies, paper continues to be an important and ubiquitous material in daily life around the world, though the ways in which we use it have shifted considerably. Altogether, we hope we have convinced—and inspired—the reader to join us in our own conviction that conserving traditional ethno-ecological knowledge is not only a professional responsibility, but an essential part of ensuring the future of Vietnamese hand papermaking and allied paper arts.

References Cited

Arcá, L. C. (2010). Traditional papermaking in Bhutan: Raw materials, techniques, and use. *International Preservation News, 52*, 37–40.

Azren, P. D., Lee, S. Y., Emang, D., & Mohamed, R. (2019). History and perspectives of induction technology for agarwood production from cultivated *Aquilaria* in Asia: A review. *Journal of Forestry Research, 30*, 1–11. https://doi.org/10.1007/s11676-018-0627-4

Barrett, T. (1983). *Japanese papermaking: Traditions, tools, and techniques.* Weatherhill.

Barrett, T. (2019). *European hand papermaking: Traditions, tools, and techniques.* Legacy Press.

Beckett, W. R. D. (1888). Streblus paper. *Bulletin of Miscellaneous Information (Royal Botanic Gardens, Kew), 15*, 81–84.

Bell, L. (1985). *Papyrus, tapa, amate, & rice paper: Papermaking in Africa, the Pacific, Latin America, and Southeast Asia.* Liliaceae Press.

Benz, B. F., López Mestas C., L., & de la Vega, J. R. (2006). Organic offerings, paper, and fibers from the Huitzilapa shaft tomb, Jalisco, Mexico. *Ancient Mesoamerica, 17*(2), 283–296. https://doi.org/10.1017/S0956536106060196

Biggs, S., & Messerschmidt, D. (2005). Social responsibility in the growing handmade paper industry of Nepal. *World Development, 33*(11), 1821–1843. https://doi.org/10.1016/j.worlddev.2005.06.002

Boesi, A. (2016). Paper plants in the Tibetan world: A preliminary study. In H. Diemberger, F.-K. Ehrhard, & P. Kornicki (Eds.), *Tibetan printing: Comparison, continuities, and change* (pp. 501–531). Brill. https://doi.org/10.1163/9789004316256_024

Boonpitaksakul, W., Chitbanyong, K., Puangsin, B., Pisutpiched, S., & Khantayanuwong, S. (2019). Natural fibers derived from Coi (*Streblus asper* Lour.) and their behavior in pulping and as paper. *BioResources, 14*(3), 6411–6420. https://doi.org/10.15376/biores.14.3.6411-6420

Bouvier, R. (1940). Le problème de la papeterie française et la solution coloniale. *Revue de botanique appliquée et d'agriculture coloniale, 226*, 381–388. https://www.persee.fr/doc/jatba_0370-3681_1940_num_20_226_1549

Cartwright, C. R., Duffy, C. M., & Wang, H. (2014). Microscopical examination of fibres used in Ming dynasty paper money. *The British Museum Technical Research Bulletin, 8*, 563–584.

Chiến H. (2020, September 13). Cao Bằng: "Hái" ra tiền từ bóc vỏ cây kỳ lạ này đem nấu thành thứ giấy vừa dai vừa bền. *Báo điện tử của Trung ương Hội Nông dân Việt Nam.* https://danviet.vn/cao-bang-hai-ra-tien-tu-boc-vo-cay-nang-sla-dem-nau-thanh-thu-giay-vua-dai-vua-ben-20200907235853308.htm?fbclid=IwAR31D7i_-BRpy-y2exWc_m634sxsaHU60dsXkAC_dl2ZQW0JVsB4fleBtLZk

Claverie, F. (1903). L'arbre à papier du Tonkin. *Bulletin economique de l'Indochine, 24,* 75–88.

Claverie, F. (1904). L'arbre à papier du Tonkin. *Bulletin economique de l'Indochine, 25,* 75–88.

Convention on International Trade in Endangered Species of Wild Fauna and Flora (CITES). (1994). *Resolutions of the Conference of the Parties. Ninth meeting of the Conference of the Parties, Fort Lauderdale, FL, USA, 7–18 November 1994.* CITES.

Crevost, C. (1907). La fabrication annamite du papier. *Bulletin Economique de l'Indochine, 60,* 789–797.

Crevost, C. (1909). Considérations sommaires sur les industries indigènes au Tonkin. *Bulletin Economique de l'Indochine, 79,* 298–327.

Crevost, C., & Lémarié, C. (1920). Catalogue des produits de l'Indochine, plantes et produits filamenteux et textiles. *Bulletin Economique de l'Indochine, 140,* 149–169.

Đỗ, Thị Thu Hiền. (2014, September 30). Nghề làm giấy bản giúp người Nùng ở Lũng Quang thoát nghèo. *Báo Điện Tử Đảng Cộng Sản Việt Nam.* https://dangcongsan.vn/xa-hoi/nghe-lam-giay-ban-giup-nguoi-nung-o-lung-quang-thoat-ngheo-270147.html

Drège, J. P. (1998). *First mentions of paper in Vietnam according to Chinese sources* (J. P. Drège, Trans.). French translation of Những ghi chép dầu tien về làm giấy ở nghề nam qua thu tịch trung hoa. *Việt Nam Học, Ký yếu Hội thảo quộc lần thứ nhất.*

Dunstan, W. R. (1904). The paper tree of Tonkin. *Bulletin of the Imperial Institute, 2,* 199–201.

Engel, P. (1994). *Origami from angelfish to zen.* Dover Publications.

Fanchette, S., & Stedman, N. (2016). *Discovering craft villages in Vietnam* (N. Stedman, Trans.). IRD Éditions, Éditions Thê Gioi. https://doi.org/10.4000/books.irdeditions.26049

Fanchette, S. (2016). Papeterie et recyclage dans les villages de métier: La fin d'un modèle de production? (Delta du fleuve Rouge, Vietnam). *Techniques & Culture, 65–66,* 1–32. http://journals.openedition.org/tc/7954

Fulling, E. (1956). Botanical aspects of the paper-pulp and tanning industries in the United States—An economic and historical survey. *American Journal of Botany, 43*(8), 621–634. https://doi.org/10.2307/2438878

Gachepapier, D., & Ševerova, D. (2019). *Paper shaping: Breathing life into origami.* Amazon.

Gary, J. (2012). Paper mulberry trees, clumps, and oval beds: The first phase of landscape restoration at Thomas Jefferson's Poplar Forest. *Magnolia, 25*(4), 1–11. https://southerngardenhistory.org/wp-content/uploads/2015/12/Magnolia_Fall_2012.pdf

Ghimire, S. K., & Nepal, B. K. (2007). *Developing a community-based monitoring system and sustainable harvesting guidelines for non-timber forest products (NTFP) in Kangchen-*

junga Conservation Area (KCA), East Nepal. World Wildlife Fund Nepal Program, Kathmandu. https://doi.org/10.13140/RG.2.2.29091.66085

Gru Hajan. (2019, November 3). Nghề Làm Giấy Truyền Thống Của Người Raglai. *Gru Hajan Dharbhan Podam.* https://gruhajan.wordpress.com/2019/11/03/nghe-lam-giay-truyen-thong-cua-nguoi-raglai/

Hà P. (2016, September 2). Vang bóng một thời giấy sắc vua ban. *Báo Quân đội nhân dân.* http://hanoi.qdnd.vn/van-hoa-the-thao/vang-bong-mot-thoi-giay-sac-vua-ban-473123

Helman-Ważny, A. (2014). A survey of Tibetan paper: History of paper in Central Asia and Tibet. In A. Helman-Ważny (Ed.), *The archaeology of Tibetan books* (pp. 179–200). Brill.

Helman-Ważny, A. (2016). Overview of Tibetan paper and papermaking: History, raw materials, techniques and fibre analysis. In O. Almogi (Ed.), *Tibetan xylograph traditions* (pp. 171–196). Department of Indian and Tibetan Studies, Universität Hamburg.

Hồng, M. (2019, August 5). Nghề giấy dó ở Khe Nghè. *Báo Dân tộc và Phát triển.* https://baodantoc.vn/nghe-giay-do-o-khe-nghe-42024.htm

Huard, P., & Durand, M. (1954). *Connaissance du Viêt-Nam.* École Française d'Extrême-Orient.

Hubbe, M. A., & Bowden, C. (2009). Handmade paper: A review of its history, craft, and science. *BioResources, 4*(4), 1736–1792. https://doi.org/10.15376/biores.4.4.1736-1792

Huett, B. (2020). The revival of Himalayan papermaking: Historical, social-cultural and economic aspects. *Z Badań Nad Książką i Księgozbiorami Historycznymi, 14*(3), 421–450. https://doi.org/10.33077/uw.25448730.zbkh.2020.632

Hunter, D. (1936). *Papermaking in Southern Siam.* Mountain House Press.

Hunter, D. (1947). *Papermaking in Indochina.* Mountain House Press.

Hunter, D. (1978). *Papermaking: The history and technique of an ancient craft* (2nd ed.). Dover.

Ilvessalo-Pfäffli, M.-S. (1995). *Fiber atlas: Identification of papermaking fibers.* Springer.

Imaeda, Y. (1989). Papermaking in Bhutan. *Acta Orientalia Academiae Scientiarum Hungaricae, 43*(2/3), 409–414.

Jeanrenaud, J. P. (1984). *Lokta (Daphne spp.) and craft paper-making in Nepal: A report on the current status, based on a literature review and preliminary field observations (May 1984–October 1984).* Forest Research and Information Centre, Forest Survey and Research Office, Department of Forest, Kathmandu, Nepal.

Jnawali, B. (2019). *Population characteristics, habitat preference and bark harvest potential of Daphne bholua in Madane Protected Forest, Gulmi, Nepal.* [Unpublished master's thesis]. Tribhuvan University.

Koretsky, E. (2003). *Traditional papermaking in Vietnam 1987 & 2000* [Video]. YouTube. https://www.youtube.com/watch?v=D2dIvoNdwec

Koretsky, E., & Koretsky, D. (1991). *The goldbeaters of Mandalay: An account of hand papermaking in Burma today.* Carriage House Press.

Laroque, C. (2020). Tonkin's giấy dó and its Chinese roots. *Z Badań Nad Książką i Księgozbiorami Historycznymi, 14*(3), 451–487. https://doi.org/10.33077/uw.25448730.zbkh.2020.633

Leandri, J. (1949). Contribution à l'étude des Thyméléacées d'Indochine. *Revue internationale de botanique appliquée et d'agriculture tropicale, 29*(323–324), 497–505. https://doi.org/10.3406/jatba.1949.6261

Lee, A. (2012). *Hanji unfurled.* Legacy Press.

Lecomte, H., Humbert, H., & Gagnepain, F. (1915). *Flore générale de l'Indochine* (Vol. 5). Masson.

León Peralta, C. E. (2023). Unfolding amate: History and innovations of an ancient paper. *The Paper, 141,* 12–13.

León Peralta, C. E., & Ojascastro, J. (2024). The sticky relationship between orchids and Mexican amate paper: Present and possible past. *Economic Botany, 78*(2). https://doi.org/10.1007/s12231-024-09608-y

Li, X., Guo, J., & Wang, B. (2015). A study of ancient paper fragments from an Eastern Han Dynasty Tomb in Minfeng County, Xinjiang Uygur Autonomous Region. *Chinese Cultural Relics, 2*(1–2), 366–370. https://dlib.eastview.com/browse/doc/45488372

Li, T. (2018). Identifying sources of fibre in Chinese handmade papers by phytoliths: A methodological exploration. *Science and Technology of Archaeological Research, 4*(1), 1–11. https://doi.org/10.1080/20548923.2018.1475454

Liu, Y., Chen, H., Yang, Y., Zhang, Z., Wei, J., Meng, H., Chen, W., Feng, J., Gan, B., Chen, X., Gao, Z., Huang, J., Chen, B., & Chen, H. (2013). Whole-tree agarwood-inducing technique: An efficient novel technique for producing high-quality agarwood in cultivated *Aquilaria sinensis* trees. *Molecules, 18*(3), 3086–3106. https://doi.org/10.3390/molecules18033086

Łuczaj, Ł. J. (2010). Plant identification credibility in ethnobotany: A closer look at Polish ethnographic studies. *Journal of Ethnobiology and Ethnomedicine, 6*(1), 1–16. https://doi.org/10.1186/1746-4269-6-36

Luo, B., Ou, Y., Pan, B., Qiu, J., & Itoh, T. (2018). The structure and development of interxylary and external phloem in *Aquilaria sinensis. IAWA Journal, 39*(1), 3–17. https://doi.org/10.1163/22941932-20170182

Mạnh, H. (2019, April 27). Còn đó giấy dó người Mường. *Nhân Dân.* https://nhandan.vn/phong-su-ky-su/con-do-giay-do-nguoi-muong-353234/

McClure, F. A. (1986). *Chinese handmade paper.* Bird and Bull Press.

Miles, L. (2019). Reviving Indonesian daluang papermaking: An interview with Tedi Permadi. *Hand Papermaking, 34*(2), 37-40.

Mullock, H. (1995). Xuan paper. *The Paper Conservator, 19*(1), 23–30. https://doi.org/10.1080/03094227.1995.9638410

Nevling, L. I. (1961). A revision of the Asiatic genus *Linostoma* (Thymelaeaceae). *Journal of the Arnold Arboretum, 42*(3), 295–320. https://doi.org/10.5962/bhl.part.19014

Nguyễn, Q. K. (2002). Rhamnoneuron balansae. In Do Dinh Sam, & Nguyen Hoang Nghia (Eds.), *Use of indigenous tree species in reforestation in Vietnam* (pp. 32–35). Forest Science Institute of Vietnam & Japan International Cooperation Agency. Agricultural Publishing House.

Nguyễn, T. B., Trần, D. L., & Nguyễn, K. K. (2007). *Vietnam red list, part II: Plants.* Science and Techniques Publishing House.

Nguyễn, T. N. (2023). Conservating and developing the giang paper making profession of the Mong ethnicity in Pa Co Commune, Mai Chau district, Hoa Binh Province. *Văn Hóa Truyền Thống Và Phát Triển, 12*(4), 84–89.

Nông, L. V. (2015, March 16). Ngôi làng 'lột xác' nhờ nghề làm giấy bản. *Báo Công An Nhân Dân.* https://cand.com.vn/Muon-mau-cuoc-song/Ngoi-lang-lot-xac-nho-nghe-lam-giay-ban-i344374/

Ojascastro, J. (2023). Prints, pleats, and preservation: Vietnamese handmade dó paper and its applications. *Guild of Book Workers Journal, 52,* 18–31.

Ojascastro, J. (2024). Of fishes, fibers, and formation aid: The dó liệt papermakers of Nghi Phong, Vietnam. *Hand Papermaking, 39*(1), 43–46.

Pang, B. (1992). *Identification of plant fibers in Hawaiian kapa: From ethnology to botany* (Publication No. 28681540). [Master's thesis, University of Hawai'i at Manoa]. ProQuest Dissertations Publishing.

Peachey, J. S. (1995). Hand papermaking in Northern Vietnam. *Hand Papermaking, 10*(1), 13–17.

Peña-Ahumada, B., Saldarriaga-Córdoba, M., Kardailsky, O., Moncada, X., Moraga, M., Matisoo-Smith, E., Seelenfreund, D., & Seelenfreund, A. (2020). A tale of textiles: Genetic characterization of historical paper mulberry barkcloth from Oceania. *PLoS ONE, 15*(5), 1–20. https://doi.org/10.1371/journal.pone.0233113

Peñailillo, J., Olivares, G., Moncada, X., Payacán, C., Chang, C.S., Chung, K.F., Matthews, P. J., Seelenfreund, A., & Seelenfreund, D. (2016). Sex distribution of paper mulberry (*Broussonetia papyrifera*) in the Pacific. *PLoS ONE, 11*(8), 1–19. https://doi.org/10.1371/journal.pone.0161148

Peters, C. M., Rosenthal, J., & Urbina, T. (1987). Otomi bark paper in Mexico: Commercialization of a pre-hispanic technology. *Economic Botany, 41*(3), 423–432. https://doi.org/10.1007/BF02859061

Phạm, P. H., Hu, C.-M., Svengsuksa, B. K. K., & Vidal, J. E. (1992). *Flore du Cambodge, du Laos, et du Vietnam. Fascicule 26: Rhoipteleaceae, Juglandaceae, Thymelaeaceae, Proteaceae. Primulaceae. Styracaceae.* Muséum national d'histoire naturelle.

Phạm, T. N. (2020, November 14). Nghề làm giấy dó của người Cao Lan: Nguy cơ thất truyền. *Báo Dân tộc và Phát triển.* https://baodantoc.vn/nghe-lam-giay-do-cua-nguoi-cao-lan-nguy-co-that-truyen-1605236262221.htm

Phạm, V. (2022). *Trúc Chỉ Studio* [Video]. University of Wisconsin - Madison Box. https://uwmadison.box.com/s/h5wgssz8aw19oog7tzlhherrm3qgia9s

Pham, V. (2023). Moments of Chây: Ecological knowledge of traditional papermaking in Viêt Nam. *Hand Papermaking, 38*(2), 20–23.

Premalatha, K., & Kalra, A. J. F. E. (2013). Molecular phylogenetic identification of endophytic fungi isolated from resinous and healthy wood of *Aquilaria malaccensis,* a red listed and highly exploited medicinal tree. *Fungal Ecology, 6*(3), 205–211. https://doi.org/10.1016/j.funeco.2013.01.005

Prendergast, H. D. V. (2002). Papyrus, paper and paper making: A view of Kew's Economic Botany Collections. *Curtis's Botanical Magazine, 19*(2), 126–144. https://doi.org/10.1111/j.1467-8748.2002.00341.x

Rantoandro, G. (1983). Contribution à la connaissance du «papier Antemoro» (Sud-est de Madagascar). *Archipel, 26*(1), 86–104. https://doi.org/10.3406/arch.1983.1847

Red Trillium Press. (2009). *Vietnam papermaking* [Video]. YouTube. https://www.youtube.com/watch?v=V2nN6DhsIgg

Richard, A. (2010). A papermaker's dilemma: Examining the use of invasive plants. *Hand Papermaking, 25*(1), 23–27.

Schattenburg-Raymond, L. (2020). A new perspective on Hawai'ian kapa-making. In F. Lennard & A. Mills (Eds.), *Material approaches to Polynesian barkcloth: Cloth, connections, communities* (pp. 73–81). Sidestone Press.

Seki, M. (2013). Database of traditional papermaking centers in East Asian regions. *Senri Ethnological Studies, 85,* 6–81. https://doi.org/10.15021/00002429

Soehartono, T., & Newton, A. C. (2000). Conservation and sustainable use of tropical trees in the genus *Aquilaria* I. Status and distribution in Indonesia. *Biological Conservation, 96*(1), 83–94. https://doi.org/10.1016/S0006-3207(00)00055-0

Soehartono, T., & Newton, A. C. (2001). Conservation and sustainable use of tropical trees in the genus *Aquilaria* II. The impact of gaharu harvesting in Indonesia. *Biological Conservation, 97*(1), 29–41. https://doi.org/10.1016/S0006-3207(00)00089-6

Subedi, B. P., Binayee, S., & Gyawali, S. (2006). *Handmade paper value chain of Nepal: prospects and challenges in growth, distributional equity and conservation.* Eleventh Conference of the International Association for the Study of Common Property. https://dlc.dlib.indiana.edu/dlc/bitstream/handle/10535/2296/Subedi_Bhishma.pdf?sequence=1&isAllowed=y

Tomasko, N. N. (2004). Chinese handmade paper—A richly varied thing. *Hand Papermaking, 19*(1), 20–32.

Trần, H. N. (2022). Dó paper: Breathing new life into an art form endangered by extinction. In R. Pandey (Ed.), *Paper and colour: Dyes and dyeing around the world* (pp. 60–77). Legacy Press.

Trần, Việt Hà. (2010). *Growth and quality of indigenous bamboo species in the mountainous regions of northern Vietnam* [Doctoral thesis, University of Göttingen]. Universitäts-bibliothek Göttingen.

Trier, J. (1972). *Ancient paper of Nepal: Results of ethno-technological fieldwork on its manu-facture, uses, and history – with technical analyses of bast, paper, and manuscripts.* Jut-land Archaeological Society Publications.

Tsien, T.-H. (2004). *Written on bamboo and silk: The Beginnings of Chinese books and inscrip-tions.* University of Chicago Press.

Tuấn, A. (2018, September 4). Giữ lửa nghề làm giấy bản. *Báo Đại Đoàn Kết.* http://daidoan-ket.vn/giu-lua-nghe-lam-giay-ban-414563.html

United Nations Educational, Scientific and Cultural Organization (UNESCO). (2003). *Con-vention for the safeguarding of the intangible cultural heritage.* https://ich.unesco.org/en/convention

von Hagen, V. (1943). *The Aztec and Maya papermakers.* J. J. Augustin.

Vũ, H. T. (2008). Amulets and the marketplace. *Asian Ethnology, 67*(2), 237–255. https://dl.ndl.go.jp/view/prepareDownload?itemId=info%3Andljp%2Fpid%2F10209972&contentNo=1

Wang Y., Gilbert, M. G., Mathew, B., Brickell, C. D., & Nevling, L. I. (2007). Thymelaeaceae. In Z. Y. Wu, P. H. Raven, & D. Y. Hong (Eds.), *Flora of China,* Vol. 13 (pp. 213–250). Missouri Botanical Garden Press.

Yadav B. D. (2000). *A five year management plan of NTFPs and Daphne of Bajura District, Nepal.* District Forest Office, Bajura.

Yatskievych, G. (2013). *Steyermark's flora of Missouri,* Vol. 3. Missouri Botanical Garden Press.

Appendix A.

Documented Extinct and Extant Papermaking Localities
in Northern Việt Nam

Village	Ward	District	Province	Latitude	Longitude	Paper Made	Extant	Ethnic Group	Source
Châm Khê	Phong Khê	Bắc Ninh City	Bắc Ninh	21.180	106.035	dó	yes	Kinh	Fanchette & Stedman 2009
Đào Xá	Phong Khê	Bắc Ninh City	Bắc Ninh	21.171	106.036	dó	yes	Kinh	Fanchette & Stedman 2009
Đống Cao	Phong Khê	Bắc Ninh City	Bắc Ninh	21.167	106.0312	dó	?	Kinh	Peachey 1995; Koretsky 2003
Dương Ổ	Phong Khê	Bắc Ninh City	Bắc Ninh	21.164	106.032	dó	yes	Kinh	Fanchette & Stedman 2009
Lũng Quang	Thông Nông	Hà Quảng	Cao Bằng	22.785	105.983	dướng	yes	Nùng	Tuấn 2018
Rìa Trên	Quốc Dân	Quảng Hòa	Cao Bằng	22.712	106.393	dướng	yes	Nùng	this publication
Suối Cỏ	Hợp Hòa	Lương Sơn	Hòa Bình	20.833	105.518	dướng	yes	Mường	this publication
n/a	Nghi Phong	Nghi Lộc	Nghệ An	18.742	105.707	dó liệt	yes	Kinh	this publication
Khe Nghè	Lục Sơn	Lục Nam	Bắc Giang	21.240	106.643	haupau	yes	Cao Lan	this publication
n/a	Việt Quang	Bắc Quang	Hà Giang	22.418	104.782	bamboo	yes	Red Dao	Phạm 2023
n/a	Hàng Kia	Mai Châu	Hòa Bình	20.742	104.875	bamboo	yes	Mông	Laroque 2020
Chà Đáy	Pà Cò	Mai Châu	Hòa Bình	20.754	104.894	bamboo	yes	Mông	Laroque 2020; Nguyễn 2023
Đông Xã	Bưởi	Tây Hồ	Hà Nội	21.048	105.811	dó	no	Kinh	Fanchette & Stedman 2009
Hồ Khẩu	Bưởi	Tây Hồ	Hà Nội	21.047	105.813	dó	no	Kinh	Fanchette & Stedman 2009
Yên Thái	Bưởi	Tây Hồ	Hà Nội	21.047	105.811	dó	no	Kinh	Hunter 1947; Peachey 1995
n/a	Nghĩa Đo	Cầu Giấy	Hà Nội	21.046	105.804	dó	no	Kinh	Huard & Durand 1954; Laroque 2020

Village	Ward	District	Province	Latitude	Longitude	Paper Made	Extant	Ethnic Group	Source
n/a	Dịch Vọng	Cầu Giấy	Hà Nội	21.035	105.793	dó	no	Kinh	Laroque 2020
Nậm Than	Liên Minh	Sa Pa	Lào Cai	22.223	104.044	bamboo	yes	White Hmong	Trần Hồng Nhung, personal communication, June 23, 2023
Suối Thầu Mông	Mường Bo	Sa Pa	Lào Cai	22.265	104.054	bamboo	yes	White Hmong	Trần Hồng Nhung, personal communication, June 23, 2023
Thạch Đê	Hiền Đa	Cẩm Khê	Phú Thọ	21.350	105.167	dó	no	?	Dunstan 1904
Phi Đình	Lang Sơn	Hạ Hòa	Phú Thọ	21.533	105.032	dó	no	?	Claverie 1903
n/a	Vân Phú	Việt Trì	Phú Thọ	21.350	105.357	dó	no	?	Claverie 1903
n/a	Vũ Yển	Thanh Ba	Phú Thọ	21.483	105.088	dó	no	?	Claverie 1903
n/a	Yên Lương	Thanh Sơn	Phú Thọ	20.992	105.250	dó	no	?	Claverie 1903

Appendix B.

Paper and papermaking tools from Việt Nam that are accessioned in the William L. Brown Center (WLBC) Biocultural Collection at the Missouri Botanical Garden in St. Louis, Missouri, USA. Further details on each of these items can be accessed online at URLs created by appending a Specimen ID to "https://tropicos.org/specimen/" (for example, the first may be accessed at https://tropicos.org/specimen/101342439). Additionally, a video describing WLBC accessions 2101, 2102, 2134, and 2136 is available here: https://youtu.be/wl_VTjjPCHo?feature=shared

Specimen ID	WLBC Accession #	Scientific Name of Plants Used	Description
101342439	2131	*Broussonetia papyrifera*	dướng paper
101342437	2130	*Linostoma persimile*	haupau paper
103432107	6936	*Linostoma persimile*	haupau phloem fiber
103430227	6921	*Maclurochloa tonkinensis*	giang paper
101342430	2136	*Magnolia* sp. *Dendrocalamus* sp.	khung seo & liềm seo
101348418	2153	*Rhamnoneuron balansae*	sắc phong paper
101342433	2134	*Rhamnoneuron balansae*	dó paper
103429895	6917	*Rhamnoneuron balansae* *Dioscorea cirrhosa*	dó paper dyed with củ nâu
101323890	2101	*Rhamnoneuron balansae*	dó votive paper
101323891	2102	*Rhamnoneuron balansae*	Đông Hồ painting
103429871	6914	*Rhamnoneuron balansae*	seashell dó paper (giấy điệp)
103433122	6944	*Rhamnoneuron balansae*	dó phloem fiber
101342440	2132	*Wikstroemia indica*	dó liệt paper
103433146	6956	*Wikstroemia indica*	dó liệt phloem fiber

Author Biographies

James Ojascastro is an ethnobotanist, papermaker, and origamist who blends science and art to inform his research and inspire his creative practice. He completed his Ph.D. in 2023 at Washington University in St. Louis in partnership with the Missouri Botanical Garden, where he studied the ecological connections between plants and people through the lens of artisanal papermaking. Currently, James lives in Georgia, where he manages field botany and plant conservation programs for the Atlanta Botanical Garden.

Veronica Y Phạm is an multidisciplinary artist, educator, and designer currently teaching at the University of Vermont. Phạm primarily works in papermaking and fiber arts in her studio practice. Her work focuses on traditional craft specific to Vietnamese and Chinese histories to connect ideas of ritual, process, labor, and identity. The materials in her work often become environmental investigations about local ecology and place-based making. Phạm continues to work with traditional and contemporary papermakers in Việt Nam with a focus on collaborative projects and research. Phạm received her MFA in Design Studies from the University of Wisconsin-Madison. She has shown her work nationally and internationally and has taught papermaking arts at the Minnesota Center for the Book, Chazen Art Museum, Zó Project, Fresh Press Paper, Southeast Asia Summer Institute, and will teach upcoming workshops at Penland School of Craft, and Ox-Bow Paper and Book Intensive.

Trần Hồng Nhung is the founder of Zó Project, a social enterprise with the mission of preserving and developing traditional papermaking in Việt Nam which has more than 800 years of history. After graduating in 2005 with a master's degree in Business Management from the IAE Aix-Marseille Graduate School of Management (France), Nhung decided to come back to Việt Nam to work for the non-profit sector to support local community development in Việt Nam. Nhung established Zó

Project with the vision to create a sustainable business as a better way to help communities in the long term. Her collaborative projects with local communities have been successful in the ecological conservation and reforestation of dó trees that use this historical fiber for traditional papermaking. She continues to work on educational projects that help connect the younger generation to preserve and pass down traditional craft knowledge.

Nhung is concerned with social, environmental, and economic development for the ethnic minority groups in Việt Nam where traditional craft practices are their sustainable livelihood. In the last 10 years, this research has led her to collaborate with traditional papermaking communities, artists, and researchers in the hopes that traditional papermaking would be recognized globally as an intangible cultural heritage craft.

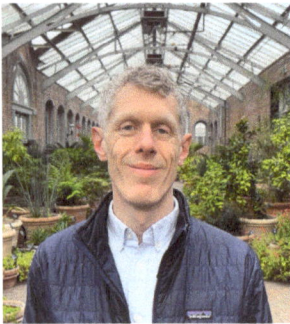

Robbie Hart is an ecologist and ethnobotanist who studies how climate change impacts plants and people. He currently leads the William L. Brown Center at Missouri Botanical Garden, a team of researchers dedicated to the study of useful plants, understanding the relationships between humans, plants, and their environment, the conservation of plant species, and the preservation of traditional knowledge for the benefit of future generations.

Glossary

baeksong The Korean word for lacebark pine, *Pinus bungeana* Zucc. ex Endl.; Pinaceae, whose wood is used to make Korean deckles (bal teul).

bal teul The wooden screen support used in Korean papermaking (webal tteugi), traditionally made from baeksong (*Pinus bungeana*).

bản A Vietnamese word for "village"; the smallest-order subnational administrative division used in Việt Nam.

báng The Vietnamese common name for a palm tree, *Arenga pinnata* (Wurmb) Merr.; Arecaceae, whose leaf fibers form the chain lines that stitch the bamboo splints in a Nùng phừ (papermaking screen) together.

bark The outermost layers of a woody plant. In papermaking, the inner layer (phloem) has the strongest fibers and yield high-quality paper, while the outer layer (cortex/black bark/green bark) is weaker, less fibrous, and sometimes used in papermaking but is more typically discarded.

bast Phloem tissue found in herbaceous plants (flax, hemp, etc.) as well as certain woody plants (kozo, dak, dó liệt, dó, etc.) composed of especially long, cellulose-rich fibers and harvested for use in fiber products like cordage, textiles, and paper.

bể seo Vat or basin used for seo papermaking techniques in Việt Nam.

bích nữ nhọn A Vietnamese common name for a vine, *Byttneria aspera* Colebr. ex Wall; Malvaceae, whose stems are cut into sections and immersed in water to make formation aid as part of Nùng and Dao Tiền papermaking traditions. Also called "mò dây" and "trôm leo" in Vietnamese and "khổ háo" in Nùng.

bìm bìm A tree, *Actinodaphne pilosa* (Lour.) Merr.; Lauraceae, whose shaved wood when immersed in water yields a mucilage used as a formation aid in dó liệt papermaking near Vinh, Việt Nam.

black bark A papermaking term referring to the outermost, usually flaky, darker-colored, and mostly dead part of bark tissue. Synonymous with "cortex."

bồ đề The Vietnamese common name for the tree *Styrax tonkinensis* (Pierre) Craib ex Hartwich; Styracaceae, whose soft and light wood is pulped in mechanical mills for making paper. It is also cultivated on plantations to provide shade for dó trees that grow in the understory. Called "*vỏ đen*" in Vietnamese.

bời lời The Vietnamese common name for a tree, *Litsea glutinosa* (Lour.) C.B.Rob.; Lauraceae, whose wood was historically shaved and soaked in water to obtain a mucilage used by Dao Tiền artisans as a formation aid to make dó paper in Đà Bắc.

bộp long One of the Vietnamese common names for *Actinodaphne pilosa* (Lour.) Merr.; Lauraceae, used as a source of mucilage to make dó liệt paper.

Cao Lan 1. An ethnic group of northeastern Việt Nam, who make and use haupau paper for divination and family records.
2. The language spoken by the Cao Lan people, which is closely related to Vietnamese.

cẩm quỳ The Vietnamese common name for *Grewia sessilifolia* Gagnep.; Malvaceae, a shrub or small tree whose phloem tissue, when immersed in water, yields a copious mucilage used as a formation aid by Cao Lan artisans to make haupau paper. Called "vạt pạ" in the Cao Lan language.

cây	The Vietnamese word for "tree."
cellulose	A carbohydrate biopolymer synthesized by plants consisting of a linear chain of β(1→4) linked D-glucose subunits, which are organized into many straw-shaped fibers that serve to maintain the structural integrity of plant cells. This is the polymer that, when liberated, isolated, concentrated, and reconstituted through the papermaking process, gives paper its strength, flexibility, and absorbency.
chả phừ	A one-piece papermaking frame made from dổi wood which supports a flexible laid bamboo screen (phừ) for Nùng papermaking. Similar in structure and design to the Korean bal teul.
chain lines	1. In a papermaking screen, the wires or threads that twine around and secure laid lines at parallel intervals. 2. The pattern of thin parallel lines left in a sheet of paper formed on a laid screen.
charge	The action of adding (or re-adding) pulp to a vat. This is periodically necessary to maintain the fiber concentration in the vat (fiber to water ratio) and thus the thickness and quality of sheets as the papermaker gradually removes pulp from the vat through repeated sheet formation and couching.
chổi lá thông	A brush, made from pine needles, that is used for adding crushed seashells to dó paper to make giấy diệp for printing Đông Hồ paintings. In Dương Ổ Village, it is used for pasting wet, pressed dó paper on concrete walls to dry fully.
chữ Hán	The Vietnamese term for Chinese characters used for writing the Chinese language.
chữ Nôm	A writing system, based on Chinese characters, formerly used for writing the Vietnamese language.
chữ Quốc ngữ	The Latin-based writing system currently used for writing the Vietnamese language.
coppicing	The practice of cutting a tree down to a stump to encourage growth of new shoots from the root collar.
cortex	A botanical term that refers to the outermost layer of bark on a woody plant; synonymous with the papermaking term "black bark."
couching	The action of transferring a newly formed, wet sheet of paper from a mould or bamboo screen and depositing it serially to form a stack of wet sheets (post). From the French verb *coucher*, "to lay down" or "to put to bed."
culm	A botanical term that refers to the aboveground stems of grasses and sedges.
dak	1. A Korean common name for a cultivated bush or small tree of hybrid origin, *Broussonetia × kazinoki* Siebold, bred from paper mulberry (*Broussonetia papyrifera*) and dwarf paper mulberry, or himekōzō (*Broussonetia monoica* Hance) and used as the principal raw material for hanji, or Korean paper. Synonymous with the Japanese word "kōzō." 2. Fibers obtained from the phloem of this tree.
Dao Tiến	An ethnic group of northwestern Việt Nam; those living in Đà Bắc District of Hòa Bình Province who harvest bark from dó trees and sell it to papermakers in Bắc Ninh.
dành dành	The Vietnamese common name for gardenia, *Gardenia jasminoides* J.Ellis, whose fruits and/or seeds have been used as a dye in Việt Nam for food and possibly also sắc phong paper.
dây trơn	A vine, scientific name unknown, claimed to be used by the Nùng people in northern Việt Nam as a source of formation aid in their papermaking tradition. Possibly synonymous with "khổ háo."
deckle	An open wooden frame that fits atop and is separable from the sieve-like mould which, by bounding the extent where pulp accumulates, determines the size and to some extent, the thickness, of the resulting sheet of paper.

điệp	The Vietnamese word for "seashell." These are crushed, mixed with fermented glutinous rice, and painted on dó paper to make printing paper (giấy in tranh) for Đông Hồ paintings.
dó	1. An understory tree, *Rhamnoneuron balansae* (Maury) Gilg; Thymelaeaceae, whose phloem tissue supplies the fibers for handmade paper. 2. Paper made from the phloem of this tree.
dó liệt	1. A shrub, *Wikstroemia indica* (L.) C.A.Mey.; Thymelaeaceae, whose phloem tissue supplies the fibers for a handmade paper used for wrapping and packaging fish in Vinh. 2. Paper made from the phloem of this shrub.
dó trầm	1. A tall tree, *Aquilaria crassna* Pierre ex Lecomte.; Thymelaeaceae, whose phloem tissue was once harvested for papermaking in Việt Nam, the Himalaya, and probably China. Many traditions involving making paper from this species are likely extinct, as the current (and often illicit) harvest of resinous heartwood from *Phialophora parasitica*-infected trees is far more economically lucrative. Thanks to a recent revival, now a minor raw material for artisanal papermaking in Sưng Village, Hòa Bình Province. 2. The Vietnamese common name for any tree belonging to the *Aquilaria* genus. 3. Vietnamese paper made from the phloem of *Aquilaria* trees.
dổi	1. The Vietnamese common name for several native tree species in the genus *Magnolia* Plum ex L. 2. The wood of these Vietnamese magnolia species, used for making khung seo and chả phừ. Volume for volume, it is four times as expensive as hinoki wood.
Đổi Mới	Lit. "renovation"; the name for Vietnamese economic reforms begun in 1986 to transition Việt Nam towards a market economy.
Đông Hồ painting	A kind of folk art on dó paper, traditionally painted but today produced as blockprints, that originates from and is still produced in the village of Đông Hồ in Bắc Ninh Province, Việt Nam. These feature iconographies reflecting themes of folk tales, social activities, astrology, and good luck.
duổi	The Vietnamese common name for Siamese roughbush (*Streblus asper* Lour.; Moraceae), whose inner bark was once used for making paper in both Thailand and Cambodia. It may have also been used for papermaking in Việt Nam, but no physical evidence of Vietnamese duổi paper exists today. Also called "khoi" in Thai.
dưỡng	1. The Vietnamese common name for *Broussonetia papyrifera* (L.) L'Hér. ex Vent.; Moraceae, a fast-growing tree whose phloem serves as the raw material for handmade paper and barkcloth across East Asia, Southeast Asia, and Oceania. Called "kajinoki" in Japan, "dak" in Korea, "daluang" in Indonesia, "saa" in Thai, and "wauke" in Hawaii. 2. Paper made from the phloem of this tree.
edge sticks	Sticks, made from wood or bamboo, sewn on one or both long edges of a bamboo screen, which serve to support and protect the integrity of the screen especially when used by papermakers as a handle when couching sheets onto posts.
fiber	A substance significantly longer than it is wide. In papermaking, these are usually hollow, plant-based, and composed almost entirely of cellulose.
flax	An annual herb, *Linum usitatissimum* L.; Linaceae, whose phloem fibers have long been used in making linen textile and for making paper either as well-worn rags, textile cuttings or new raw flax fiber.

float mould	A type of pour mould composed of a porous screen stretched taut across a rigid, buoyant frame. Before sheet formation, it is floated in a vat of water such that the interior floods and the screen is fully submerged. A well-mixed suspension of water, pulp, and formation aid is then poured into the flooded interior of the float mould and whisked around until the fiber is uniformly distributed above the submerged screen. Sheets are then formed by carefully raising the float mould out of the vat, allowing water to drain and the pulp to deposit on the screen as a wet sheet of paper. The float moulds are then left in the sun to allow the paper to dry directly on the screen. Not known to be used in Việt Nam today, but still used extensively in Himalayan papermaking traditions.
formation aid	A mucilage used in hand papermaking traditions to reduce clumping between fibers, improve fiber dispersion in the vat and on the screen, and slow water drainage from the screen.
gáo nước	The Vietnamese word for a shrub, possibly the buttonbush *Cephalanthus tetrandra* (Roxb.) Ridsdale & Bakh.f.; Rubiaceae, whose bark, when immersed in water, yields a mucilage used as a formation aid in Đống Cao Village, Bắc Ninh Province, Việt Nam. Its use for this purpose may no longer be extant.
giấy	The Vietnamese word for "paper."
giấy bản	1. Paper sheets, of any kind. 2. Copy paper; can be used to refer to mid-grade dó paper used for this purpose. 3. A term to describe the kind of paper made from dướng fiber by the Nùng ethnic group in Cao Bằng Province, Việt Nam.
giấy điệp	Lit. "seashell paper"; the Vietnamese term for dó paper that is treated on one side with a slurry of fermented sticky rice and pulverized seashells to make a white, ink-receptive surface for Đông Hồ paintings.
giấy in tranh	Lit. "painting paper"; the Vietnamese term for paper suitable for painting or printing (e.g., Đông Hồ paintings).
giấy khan	The Vietnamese term for packaging paper; can refer to mid-grade dó paper used for this purpose.
giấy thủ công	The Vietnamese term for handmade paper.
gỗ	The Vietnamese word for "wood."
green bark	A papermaking term referring to the middle layer of bark in between the white bark (innermost layer, or phloem) and the black bark (outermost layer, or cortex). Often called "green" due to the presence of chlorophyll in the thin, living part of this layer. Called "*vỏ xanh*" in Vietnamese.
hachiku	The Japanese common name for henon, *Phyllostachys nigra* var. *henonis* (Mitford) Rendle, a bamboo whose culms are carefully split and shaped into splints and used for constructing su (Japanese papermaking screens).
haupau	1. The Cao Lan common name for a liana, *Linostoma persimile* Craib; Thymelaeaceae, whose phloem tissue supplies the fibers for a handmade paper made by the Cao Lan people in northeastern Việt Nam. 2. Paper made from the phloem of this liana.
henon	A bamboo, *Phyllostachys nigra* var. *henonis* (Mitford) Rendle, whose culms are carefully split and shaped into splints and used for constructing su (Japanese papermaking screens). Called "hachiku" in Japanese.
hồ	The Vietnamese word for "starch," regardless of its vegetable origin. Starch from cassava (sắn) is mixed with water to make a starch solution (nước hồ) to paste stacks of dó to concrete walls in Bắc Ninh as part of the drying process.
hòe	The Vietnamese common name for the pagoda tree, *Styphnolobium japonicum* (L.) Schott; Fabaceae, whose flower was once used as a source of dye to make yellow sắc phong paper.

Hollander beater	A mechanical, motor-powered beater consisting of a racetrack-shaped basin for channeling fiber slurry, a cylindrical rotor mounted with straight, sharpened blades around its circumference, and a bedplate mounted beneath the rotor, itself fitted with a set of closely spaced vertical bars. This beater, with its blades oriented perpendicular to the flow of slurry, is designed to cut and fibrillate fibers as they flow around the basin. The space between the rotor and the bedplate bars can be adjusted to change the degree and rate of beating action.
hu đay	The Vietnamese common name for gunpowder tree, *Trema orientale* (L.) Blume; Cannabaceae, which grows in Đà Bắc District and could show promise as a new raw material for revived Dao Tiền hand papermaking traditions.
huyên	The Vietnamese word for "district"; a rural subnational administrative division in Việt Nam that is larger than a commune (xã) and smaller than a province (tỉnh).
inner bark	The papermaker's term for the phloem tissue of woody plants whose bast fiber is used in papermaking; excludes the darker, flakier "black bark" or "green bark" which covers the inner bark while the plant is alive.
keo	The Vietnamese word for "glue." Used here in reference to white (polyvinylacetate) glue used as a sizing by origami artists in Việt Nam to render dó and dưỡng paper suitable as a folding medium.
keta	The Japanese word for their deckle and lower mould frame that are hinged together like a clamshell. It is latched in place around a flexible laid bamboo screen (su) and used in Japanese nagashizuki hand papermaking (the two together are termed a *sugeta*). Analog of the Vietnamese khung seo and Korean bal teul.
khổ háo	The Nùng term for a vine, *Byttneria aspera* Colebr. ex Wall; Malvaceae, whose stems are cut into sections and immersed in water to make formation aid as part of Nùng papermaking traditions. Also called "bích nữ nhọn," "mò dây," and "trôm leo" in Vietnamese.
khoi	The Thai common name for Siamese roughbush (*Streblus asper* Lour.; Moraceae), whose inner bark was once used for making paper in both Thailand and Cambodia, and possibly also in Việt Nam. Also called "duối" in Vietnamese.
khung seo	The Vietnamese term for their two-part bamboo deckle made from dổi wood which holds a flexible laid bamboo screen (liêm seo) in place in Vietnamese papermaking. Vietnamese analog of the Japanese keta.
Kinh	The dominant ethnic group in Việt Nam, representing about 85% of its population.
kōzō	1. A Japanese common name for a cultivated bush or small tree of hybrid origin, *Broussonetia × kazinoki* Siebold, bred from paper mulberry (*Broussonetia papyrifera*) and dwarf paper mulberry, or himekōzō (*Broussonetia monoica* Hance), and used as the principal raw material for washi, or Japanese paper. Synonymous with the Korean word "dak." 2. Fibers obtained from the phloem of this tree.
kraing	The Khmer name for manuscripts composed of sheets of paper—usually made from either *Broussonetia papyrifera* or *Streblus asper* fibers—pasted together and folded like an accordion.
laid lines	1. On a screen, the parallel array of splints that support a newly formed sheet of paper before it is couched. 2. The pattern of thick parallel lines left on sheet of paper formed on a laid mould.
laid mould	A mould whose screen is constructed from sturdy splints (laid lines) woven together with wire, thread, horsehair, or silk (chain lines).
lể	The Vietnamese word for cooked and beaten papermaking fiber prior to sheet formation.
liêm seo	A bamboo screen used in Vietnamese papermaking, composed of thin, parallel bamboo splints woven together with thread, horsehair, or (today) monofilament. Vietnamese analog of the Japanese su.

lignin	A biopolymer with an irregular chemical structure synthesized by plants and responsible for the structural integrity and decay resistance of wood. In papermaking, although largely removed during cooking and rinsing, residual lignin can contribute to making paper brittle and darkened in color over time.
lime	An alkaline, calcium-based material (calcium oxide or calcium hydroxide) ultimately of mineral origin and used as an aqueous reagent to chemically separate vegetable fibers during the hand papermaking process. Lime is obtained by burning chalk (calcium carbonate; $CaCO_3$) in a kiln, which yields quicklime or unslaked lime (calcium oxide; CaO). Quicklime can in turn be further processed by the addition of water to yield slaked lime (calcium hydroxide; $Ca(OH)_2$). Either quicklime or slaked lime may be used when cooking raw fiber to assist in fiber separation.
lokta	1. The Nepali common name for a shrub, *Daphne bholua* Buch.-Ham. ex D.Don; Thymelaeaceae, whose phloem fiber is the predominant raw material for hand papermaking traditions across the Himalaya.
	2. The Nepali common name for a related shrub, *Daphne papyracea* Wall. ex G.Don; Thymelaeaceae, whose phloem fiber is also harvested for papermaking across the Himalaya.
	3. Himalayan handmade paper, especially that made from either *Daphne bholua* or *Daphne papyracea* (but sometimes also *Edgeworthia gardneri* Meisn.; Thymelaeaceae) phloem.
may sla	A Nùng common name for the dướng tree.
mảy tàn	The Nùng common name for *Phyllostachys edulis* (Carrière) J.Houz.; Poaceae, a bamboo whose culms are split, shaved into splints, and tied together to make phừ (Nùng papermaking screens). Also called "trúc sào" in Vietnamese.
mazé	In Japanese papermaking, a comb-like structure that is mounted above a vat such that its long wooden teeth are partially immersed in the slurry of fiber, water, and formation aid. This tool is swung rapidly back and forth to whisk fibers in the vat and disperse them uniformly immediately prior to nagashizuki sheet formation.
mò	1. The Vietnamese common name for the tree *Litsea monopetala* (Roxb.) Pers., whose wood is shaved and soaked in water to obtain a mucilage used as formation aid to make dó paper in Bắc Ninh. Historically misidentified as *Clerodendrum* or a variety of different species in the genus *Litsea*.
	2. The mucilage obtained from the wood of this plant.
	3. Any mucilage used as formation aid in Vietnamese hand papermaking.
mò dây	A Vietnamese common name for a vine, *Byttneria aspera* Colebr. ex Wall; Malvaceae, whose stems are cut into sections and immersed in water to make formation aid as part of Nùng and Dao Tiền papermaking traditions. Also called "bích nữ nhọn" and "trôm leo" in Vietnamese and "khổ háo" in Nùng.
mould	The essential tool in hand papermaking, consisting of a porous screen on which fiber is deposited.
Mường	1. The third-largest ethnic group in Việt Nam, who live primarily in the foothills and mountains west of Hà Nội, and who have had a tradition making paper by hand from dướng bark that persisted up until the mid-20th century, went extinct, and was revived again in 2006.
	2. The language spoken by the Mường people, which is closely related to Vietnamese.
nagashizuki	A method of sheet formation used in Japan for making large quantities of paper by hand from long bast fibers. This technique is characterized by energetic movements by the papermaker, usage of a mould with a clamshell frame (keta), multiple vigorous vat charges onto a bamboo screen, usage of a viscous formation aid for fiber dispersion, and couching without interleaving felts between sheets. Japanese analog of Vietnamese seo.

naginata beater A mechanical, motor-powered beater consisting of a racetrack-shaped basin for channeling fiber slurry and a rotor armed with a staggered array of usually un-sharpened (sometimes sharpened), sickle-shaped blades. This beater, with its blades oriented parallel to the flow of slurry, is designed to separate and disperse, rather than cut, fibers as they flow around the basin.

năng sla A Nùng term for the dướng (*Broussonetia papyrifera*) tree.

nghệ The Vietnamese word for turmeric (*Curcuma longa* L.; Zingiberaceae), whose yellow rhizome was once used by the Lại family papermakers for dyeing sắc phong paper until the mid-1940s.

nghiến
1. The Vietnamese common name for a tree, *Burretiodendron hsienmu* W.Y.Chun & F.C.How; Malvaceae, whose hard brown wood is fashioned into mallets and beating surfaces to manually pulp dướng phloem fibers according to Nùng papermaking traditions.
2. Wood from this tree.

Nùng
1. An ethnic group of northern Việt Nam and southern China; those living in Thông Nông District of Cao Bằng Province make paper by hand from dướng trees.
2. A language in the Tai-Kadai language family spoken by this ethnic group.

nước hồ The Vietnamese phrase for a starch solution. Used to paste stacks of damp, pressed sheets of dó to concrete walls as part of the drying process.

ổi The Vietnamese word for guava, *Psidium guajava* L.; Myrtaceae, whose hard wood is used to make mallets for beating dướng and dó fiber.

outer bark In woody plants, the external layers of bark, excluding the phloem. Consists of "green bark" and "black bark."

phloem Plant stem vascular tissue, located between the bark and xylem, and used by plants to transport the sugars made in photosynthesis to the rest of the plant. A common (though not exclusive) source of pliable, cellulose-rich fiber used in many traditions around the world for cordage, textiles, and paper.

phử A bamboo screen used in Nùng papermaking, composed of thin, parallel bamboo splints woven together with báng (*Arenga pinnata*) fibers, and onto which pulped paper mulberry phloem fibers are formed into sheets.

post A stack of newly-formed sheets of paper on to which additional sheets are subsequently couched.

pour mould A tool used in hand papermaking that allows sheet formation to occur by pouring a fiber slurry onto its screen. In Việt Nam, it is used in the manufacture of dó liet and haupau paper.

pueblos mágicos Towns in Mexico that are recognized by the Mexican Tourism Secretariat to have cultural, historical, culinary, and/or artisanal significance.

ramie An herbaceous perennial, *Boehmeria nivea* (L.) Gaudich.; Urticaceae, whose phloem fibers have been used for coarse textiles and the earliest papers.

ràng The Mường word for the dướng (*Broussonetia papyrifera*) tree.

recalcitrant In botany, refers to seeds or pollen that remain viable for only a short time (i.e., they cannot be stored long-term).

ribs Long, thin pieces of wood with a wedge-shaped cross section made of various species of tree or bamboo that are oriented parallel to one another and fixed in the interior space of a papermaking frame or mould. These are designed to support from underneath, either a removable bamboo screen (in Eastern papermaking traditions) or the wire mesh of a mould (in Western papermaking traditions).

saa The Thai common name for paper mulberry, *Broussonetia papyrifera* (L.) L'Hér. ex Vent.; Moraceae, used as a raw material for papermaking throughout Southeast Asia, including Việt Nam. Also called "dướng" in Vietnamese and "ràng" in Mường.

sắc phong	A type of expensive and high-quality yellow dó paper that was traditionally used by the Vietnamese royal court. It was made by the Lại family from the mid-17th century until 1944. The requisite yellow dye may be extracted from a variety of plant sources, including from hòe (*Styphnolobium japonicum*) flowers and gardenia seeds. Today, sắc phong is made by the Phạm family, who dye the sheets by airbrushing with yellow food coloring.
samut	The Thai name for manuscripts composed of sheets of paper—usually made from either saa (*Broussonetia papyrifera*) or khoi (*Streblus asper*) fibers—pasted together and folded like an accordion.
sắn	The Vietnamese word for cassava, *Manihot esculenta* Crantz; Euphorbiaceae, whose edible tuberous root is the source of starch (hồ), which, when dissolved in water, is used to adhere stacks of dó paper on the wall for drying.
screen	The porous part of a papermaking mould, on which fiber is deposited and through which water and formation aid drain during sheet formation.
seo	A method of sheet formation used in Việt Nam for making large quantities of dó and dướng paper. This technique is characterized by smooth and nimble but tempered movements by the papermaker, usage of a papermaking mould with a fully separable two-part frame (khung seo), 2–4 vat dips onto a bamboo screen, delicate usage of a viscous formation aid for fiber dispersion, and couching without interleaving felts between sheets.
soda ash	Another name for sodium carbonate (Na_2CO_3), which is used as an aqueous reagent to chemically separate vegetable fibers in the manufacture of haupau (and other kinds of handmade) paper.
su	The Japanese word for a bamboo screen used in nagashizuki papermaking, composed of thin, parallel bamboo splints woven together with silk threads or sometimes synthetic alternatives like nylon. Analog of the Vietnamese liềm seo and Korean bal.
Tết	A major holiday in Việt Nam, corresponding to the first day of the lunar New Year.
thành phố	The Vietnamese word for "city"; an urban subnational administrative division in Việt Nam that is larger than a commune (xã) and smaller than a province (tỉnh).
tỉnh	The Vietnamese word for "province"; the first-order subnational administrative division used in Việt Nam today.
Tonkin	1. The French name for the region encompassing northern Việt Nam. 2. The name of the protectorate encompassing what is now northern Việt Nam and controlled by France as part of French Indochina from 1883–1945 and again from 1945–1948.
tororo-aoi	A shrub, *Abelmoschus manihot* (L.) Medik.; Malvaceae, whose root is harvested for mucilage used as a formation aid in Japanese and Korean papermaking. Called "hwangchokgyu" in Korean.
tre	A Vietnamese common name for an unknown bamboo species used to make the thin splints of liềm seo.
trôm leo	A Vietnamese common name for a vine, *Byttneria aspera* Colebr. ex Wall; Malvaceae, whose stems are cut into sections and immersed in water to make formation aid as part of Nùng papermaking traditions. Also called "bích nữ nhọn" and "mò dây" in Vietnamese and "khổ háo" in Nùng.
Trúc Chỉ	Modern Vietnamese paper art as interpreted and pioneered by Phan Hải Bằng at his studio in Huế.

Trucchigraphy	A paper art methodology that bridges traditional papermaking techniques, the water-blowout technique, and principles from printmaking to create works of art that reveal layers of imagery on an illuminated surface. Like the idea of calligraphy, Trucchigraphy was created to emphasize the painterly use of the contemporary art form, Trúc Chỉ.
trúc sào	The Vietnamese common name for *Phyllostachys edulis* (Carrière) J.Houz.; Poaceae, a bamboo whose culms are split, shaved into splints, and tied together to make phừ (Nùng papermaking screens). Also called "mây tàn" in Nùng.
vải thiều	The Vietnamese common name for lychee, *Litchi sinensis* J.F.Gmel.; Sapindaceae, whose wood is shaved and soaked in water to extract an orange-brown dye used by Mường papermakers for coloring dướng paper.
vạt pạ	The Cao Lan common name for *Grewia sessilifolia* Gagnep.; Malvaceae, a shrub or small tree whose phloem tissue, when immersed in water, yields a copious mucilage used as a formation aid by Cao Lan artisans to make haupau paper. Called "cẩm quỷ" in Vietnamese.
vỏ	The Vietnamese word for bark (as of a tree).
vỏ đen	The Vietnamese translation of "black bark."
vỏ trắng	The Vietnamese translation of "white bark."
vỏ xanh	The Vietnamese translation of "green bark."
wangdae	The Korean common name for *Phyllostachys reticulata* (Rupr.) K.Koch; Poaceae, a bamboo whose culms are split, shaved into splints, and tied together with monofilament to make bal (Korean papermaking screens).
washi	The Japanese word for Japanese paper, usually made by hand from the phloem fibers of kōzō (*Broussonetia ×kazinoki* Siebold; Moraceae), though other fibers, including **mitsumata** (*Edgeworthia chrysantha* Lindl.; Thymelaeaceae) and **gampi** (*Wikstroemia sikokiana* Franch. & Sav.; Thymelaeaceae) may be used.
water blowout technique	A technique using controlled water pressure to gently move pulp on a screen or mould away from a two-dimensional stencil or cutout.
webal tteugi	A sheet formation technique indigenous to the Korean Peninsula, where a large screen (bal) and support (bal teul) are manipulated at opposite ends by a papermaker and a suspended rope, and then dipped from side to side (yupmuljil) into a vat of fiber, water, and formation aid underneath. This technique is not practiced in Việt Nam.
white bark	A papermaking term referring to the innermost, pale-colored, and usually fibrous layer of bark belonging to the stem of a woody plant. Synonymous with "bast" and "phloem." Called "*vỏ trắng*" in Vietnamese.
wood	Lignified xylem of perennial plants.
wove mould	A mould whose screen is made of a mesh or woven material, such as wire, silk, cotton, or mosquito netting; paper made from these moulds will lack both chain lines and laid lines when viewed in transmitted light.
xã	The Vietnamese word for "commune"; a subnational administrative division in Việt Nam that is larger than a village (xóm) and smaller than a district (huyên).
xóm	A Vietnamese word for "village"; the smallest-order subnational administrative division used in Việt Nam.
xylem	Dead vascular tissue in the stem of a plant that conducts water from the roots to the leaves. In most plants with perennial stems, the xylem becomes lignified and is called wood.
yupmuljil	The Korean term for the arcing movements where a papermaker repeatedly dips a Korean bamboo screen (bal) and screen support (bal teul) together as a unit from side to side in and out of a vat filled with water and pulp as part of Korean sheet formation (webal tteugi).

www.ingramcontent.com/pod-product-compliance
Lightning Source LLC
Chambersburg PA
CBHW060801270326
41926CB00002B/53